Sold On Short Term Rentals

How to Buy, Launch and Manage Your First Cash Flowing Property

Paige Miller

Sold On Short Term Rentals

How to Buy, Launch and Manage Your First Cash Flowing Property

Paige Miller

Copyright © 2023 Reflek

All Rights Reserved.

No part of this publication may be reproduced, distributed, or transmitted in any form or by any means, including photocopying, recording, or other electronic or mechanical methods, without the prior written permission of the publisher, except in the case of brief quotations embodied in critical reviews and certain other noncommercial uses permitted by copyright law.

Disclaimer: The author makes no guarantees concerning the level of success you may experience by following the advice and strategies contained in this book, and you accept the risk that results will differ for each individual. The purpose of this book is to educate, entertain, and inspire.

For more information: book@thepaigemiller.com

Paperback ISBN: 978-1-962280-00-6
EBOOK ISBAN: 978-1-962280-01-3

Get your FREE resources here:
SCAN

My Gift to YOU Includes:
Must-Have Inventory List
Questions To Ask Your CPA
ROI Calculator
Renovation Calculator
Property Description Sample
Tips on Partnerships
Mentorship Opportunities

Dedication

To My Dad: My muse. My desire to write a book was born out of the lessons I learned about life and the realizations I encountered during the early weeks and months after you passed on. I know you have been alongside me for this whole journey and nothing has felt more aligned since you've been gone. Thank you for the inspiration. Your magic lives on.
With love, The Sand Fairy

Table of Contents

Preface 7

Introduction: What This Is All About 11
    Chapter 1: So, You Think You Want To Own
    A Short Term Rental? 13
    Chapter 2: So, Why Learn From Me? 19
    Chapter 3: Here Is How It Will Work 29

Part 1: Let's Buy This Thing 33
    Chapter 4: How To Choose Your Market 35
    Chapter 5: What To Buy 47
    Chapter 6: The Financial Position to Succeed 59
    Chapter 7: The Deal 67

Part 2: Let's Get Geared Up 75
    Chapter 8: Cast Your Vision 77
    Chapter 9: Own Your Role 81
    Chapter 10: To Self-Manage or Not To Self-Manage,
    That Is The Question 87

Chapter 11: Meet The Team 91
Chapter 12: Outfitting The Space 99
Chapter 13: This Is How We Do It 109
Chapter 14: Ready to Launch 113

Part 3: Let's Make Some Money 119
Chapter 15: Managing Reservations 121
Chapter 16: You Are In Hospitality, After All 133
Chapter 17: From Zero To Superhost 139
Chapter 18: Hosting Secrets For Lasting Results 145
Chapter 19: The Mountains On Your Horizon 151
Chapter 20: It's Time To Take The Reins 157

Let's Connect: 161
Shout Outs 163
Leave A Review! 165
About Paige 167

Preface

My Journey Here

Becoming an Author has not been a life-long aspiration of mine. In fact, I never considered myself a writer. Growing up, I really didn't enjoy school or reading and I never felt like I excelled in academics, so it never crossed my mind. Since I didn't have the desire to, why would I have any business writing a book?

As an adult, I really leaned into journaling to sort through my thoughts and manage anxiety. At the beginning of 2022, my Dad unexpectedly and suddenly passed away. It completely rocked my world and changed our family as a whole.

He was the guy that everyone loved. Dad was interesting, educated, a philosopher and poet in his own right, an outdoorsman, and an avid reader. His party trick was reciting Robert Service poems while enjoying some brandy or the like.

When I was growing up, my Dad created an alter ego for me that he named "The Sand Fairy." It was my creative and powerful outlet to be connected to my inner wisdom. Alignment without boundaries, if you will. Immediately after his passing, I was instantly transformed into a headspace of connection with this long-lost character within me. I went on a self-discovery journey and landed on this idea of becoming an author and actually writing a book. I knew that I had wisdom to share, so I felt very aligned with the goal of writing to share my message.

Thanks to the power of social media, I was connected with Jake Kelfer on Instagram. It was Thanksgiving weekend and we were enjoying the holiday in snowy Montana when I decided to take the leap and sign up for his book writing workshop in LA. I had NO IDEA what I was doing or what to expect and I was nervous to attend, but I also knew that I had a calling to go. So off to Los Angeles I went in March of 2023 to embark on my journey to *Sold On Short Term Rentals*.

This book is much more than a product to me. It has come from my soul. Yes, it is a non-fiction how-to on real estate investing, which may seem anything but soulful, but to me it is. Real estate has been the center of my universe since 2011. I have built my career around it, my family around it, and my retirement around it. As much as my life is also about fun and family, it is all tied into real estate.

So, as you come along on this journey with me, know that this book has been written to help you connect to all that is possible in your life. Consider how the power of real estate can be your vehicle, as it has been mine. As you read through this book, I hope that it gives you a realistic view into the world of real estate investing. You will see what it actually looks like to be an active investor and whether or not that will be a good fit for you. Maybe you will decide that short term rentals aren't for you, but that another type of real estate investment is.

My goal is to offer you a book that helps you feel like you have enough information to go and do this yourself. Your way may be different than mine, but hopefully your takeaway will be, "If Paige can do it, so can I," and that is great! You can do this! And though I am the expert in my own way of buying, launching, and managing our rentals, I understand if it won't be the perfect fit for everyone who reads this.

Preface

Or maybe you are already a short term rental investor and you do things differently. Great! Maybe you will learn how to implement some of my theories into your current business. Another possibility is that you own a vacation rental that is handled by a property management company and you want to move into self-management. Or maybe you are just really interested in getting started but don't know how. This book is for anyone who wants to start, optimize their current systems, or manage their rental themselves. Regardless of your unique situation, I hope that this book sparks your interest and grows your understanding of how impactful real estate ownership is.

Introduction:
What This Is All About

Chapter 1:
So, You Think You Want To Own A Short Term Rental?

The sexiest real estate investment that you can make is a short term rental. Why? Well, picture this: You have a home full of style and comfort that is not only something you are proud of but also represents you and your unique contribution to the short term rental market. On top of that, it brings you additional income and opportunities.

The number one reason why people get into short term rentals is to have a higher rate of cash flow up front while still capitalizing on the long term benefits of owning real estate. Most people interested in short term rental investing have a dream of delivering a high-quality home for guests to enjoy because they have a deep desire to provide a property that they would want to rent. People want to make a good investment while also experiencing the excitement and perceived fun that comes from hosting people in a specifically curated space.

So let me guess, your problem is that you dream of owning a short term rental or two, but you have no idea where to start, what is actually involved, how to buy a property, what to look for, or how to run it effectively. Is it actually attainable for someone like you?

Real estate investing is powerful. I highly recommend that everyone owns real estate because the doors that it can unlock for you financially are second to none, in my humble opinion. Full disclosure, I am in real estate sales meaning that I am a realtor, so I really am passionate about all of the ways that real estate can change lives.

If you are reading this book, you already know this on some level—maybe just from hearing about your parents' insane amount of equity from the house they bought in 1989 that is now worth five times as much, or maybe because you have friends with a rental, or maybe since you are just an HGTV junky. Who doesn't love a good gut renovation project turned into a masterpiece in the span of an hour? Maybe you already have a long term rental and you are curious about short term rentals. Can they really cashflow that much? Aren't they such a pain with all of the guests, turnover, complaints, and things breaking or going missing? I am here to set the record straight on ALL of those things. I also live up to my name because I am an open book and I am about to show you the behind-the-scenes on how my husband and I have gone from flipping dirt for investments to owning and managing multiple vacation rentals.

First: WHAT a short term rental is:

Let's identify exactly what constitutes a short term rental. For me, and in most markets, a rental that is offered for stays from 1-28 days is considered a short term rental. It is important to understand this so that you are clear on what potential local restrictions and permits may be required in your chosen market. This also means that you will oversee far more turnover between guests than your traditional long term rental with lease contracts that last six months to a year at a time or more. That being said, short term rentals require more time management in order to get the house ready between guests. With more problems comes more money. Wait! Did I say that wrong? Okay, jokes aside, my point is that with a higher return investment comes a set of new challenges. You get paid the big bucks for a reason.

Second: Here are the BENEFITS of a short term rental:

There are many benefits to choosing to become a short term rental investor and I want to make sure I paint an accurate picture of what this kind of ownership truly looks like to help you make sure this is right for you. Let me tell you, it is awesome! I love being a short term rental investor and host. It suits our lifestyle, desire, and skillset, which means that we are fulfilled on many levels. From planning for retirement to enjoying our vacation homes along the way, we feel like we are in control of our future by the degree of hustle that we invest in our properties.

As I mentioned before, most people are drawn into the STR market by having the ability to fetch higher cash flow rates. Instead of bringing in $200-$500 per month with a long term rental, you have the opportunity to cash flow thousands of dollars a month time and time again. I will show you the exact road map of how to produce that outcome for yourself by demonstrating the proper way to purchase, outfit, launch, and manage your rental. Let's be clear, gone are the days of throwing up a picture of your living room couch and getting guests to book their stay at your place. The bar has been raised and it is so critical to make sure that you deliver for your guests in order to get those coveted returns on investment. And guess what? It is simple! All you have to do is follow the process and the results will be waiting for you on the other side.

Not only is there the benefit of higher monthly returns, but you still get the same long term benefits of owning real estate. If you are reading this, you likely have a day job at the moment. What you may not realize is that your short term rental can help you off-set your current tax burden by allowing you a whole host—pun intended—of potential tax write-offs and credits. Full disclosure, I am not a tax professional but

I do know the power of real estate when it comes to tax season. Just by owning real estate, you are eligible to write off things like mortgage interest, supplies for your rental business, repair and maintenance costs, and utilities.

> **Spoiler Alert:**
> As soon as you cross over from being an employee to a business owner, gone are the days of Turbo Tax. You need to hire a tax professional who will help you prepare for tax season by tracking certain things throughout the year. You can even write off mileage for traveling to your rental as long as you are going for some maintenance and repairs, but you might as well pack a bag and stay a couple of nights while you're at it!
>
> Scan the QR code at the beginning of the book for the free list of questions to ask!

Your short term rental is going to give you the ability to create a space that is uniquely you and that you are proud to share with the world. On a smaller scale, it will be a place where you get to invite your loved ones to come and enjoy with you—for free.

If you have been daydreaming about having a short term rental, then you or your partner likely have the desire to be in hospitality and deliver a high-level experience for your future guests. The powerful thing about having a short term rental is that it can be the gateway to a much larger hospitality business. I have seen many people start with having one or two vacation rentals and, once they understand the process of being successful, they set their sights on buying a boutique hotel or motel to deliver the same excellent experience for travelers on a larger scale. The possibilities with the short term rental space are endless.

But where do you start? The number one thing holding you back from starting your short term rental journey is that you don't know where or how to start. For many, the idea of buying and running a short term rental is a really cool dream but making it a reality is still a distant desire. I am here to tell you that if I can do it then so can you. The key to doing anything in life is to start, and this book will give you the tactical step-by-step process to go from analysis paralysis to Superhost. All you have to do is *the work*.

Chapter 2:
So, Why Learn From Me?

What gives me the authority to write this book and give advice on how to be a successful short term rental owner? Well, I am a successful short term rental owner and I have now replicated this process multiple times over, both for myself and for others.

I first started in real estate investing because I got into real estate sales in 2011 when I was fresh out of undergrad. I graduated from the University of Washington, Tacoma, and was on the path of applying for sales jobs in Seattle and Bellevue. Every time I would leave an interview, I was like, "Man, this just is not feeling right." So, I came home and hopped on Craigslist, as one did in 2011, to search for jobs. I focused on looking in the real estate space. I had it in my mind that I wanted to eventually end up in real estate, but I also had this notion that I needed to be older, well-established financially, and have some other type of real-world success before embarking on that career path. Boy, was I wrong.

I ended up landing a full-time position as an assistant transaction coordinator for the number one real estate team in my hometown. After only a few weeks, the owner of the team made it very clear that I wasn't exactly killing it in this role. As it turns out, administrative roles are not the best suited for my skill set. So, they gave me another opportunity by offering to help me get my real estate license and try out sales.

I got my license in record time and was off to the races. I sold 30 homes in my first year, and so I knew that this was the career for me. I also learned a ton about the power of real estate. Keep in mind that this was in 2011, so the Great Recession and real estate crash were still very real and felt ever-present. Many of my transactions were short sales and foreclosures, so I learned a valuable lesson as a young realtor and future investor by seeing the aftermath of over-leveraging yourself very early on. While the market was still raw from the wounds of 2008, the real estate market was actually on the upward climb toward recovery.

It was two years before I would buy my first house. To this day, I wish that I had bought as many homes as I could afford during my first two years in the business, but hindsight is always 20/20 and every past market is the one that you should have bought in. Trust me. So, my professional advice is to buy the damn real estate.

My first home purchase was in the Chicago suburbs. Before I talk about that, I must introduce you to my husband, Jeff. At the time that we purchased this home, we weren't yet married. In fact, we weren't even engaged but we were moving toward Jeff attending graduate school, so we purchased our first house within a few minutes of his school campus. It was a cute little 1950s Cape Cod-style home with many quirks and a great fenced-in backyard. We were in a pocket of an affordable neighborhood and surrounded by homes that were three to five times more expensive than ours.

The fun part about this purchase, aside from the excitement of it being our first, was that we were shopping for homes virtually before shopping for homes virtually was even a thing! Our realtor would go and take videos, upload them to her computer, and then email them over for us to watch. This was seven years before the pandemic. Talk about being progressive! After several virtual tours, we finally decided to make an offer on a home, sight unseen. After some negotiations, we were under contract! Jeff flew out for the home inspection and everything looked as we expected, so we moved forward to closing. It was August when we left Washington for our new four-year home in Illinois.

This home ended up being our first investment property. We put some sweat equity into it and, at the end of our time in the Midwest, we were able to walk away with a profit. Not to mention, we saved a lot of money by not throwing away monthly rent payments. I always looked at it as a forced savings account for several reasons.

+ First, because of our down payment. This is the money that we were putting into our house upfront that when we went to sell it we would likely get it back.
+ Second, our monthly payments had a portion going to paying down our loan amount—I could have said principal balance, but let's not overcomplicate things—which just kept stacking the amount of money that we would likely get back once we went to sell in the future.
+ And third, market appreciation made our nest egg at the end even bigger through equity. That is where the real magic happens in real estate.

When I did the rent versus own calculation back in 2016—yes, I still have it filed away—it was saving us $39,403.03 per year compared to what other graduate students who were renting were paying. That figure included tax benefits, not just rent payments. Not to mention, we had all the perks from our "forced savings account," a place where we could put down roots for the whole duration of Jeff's four-year program, and the ability to paint, decorate, and improve our house as we wanted. Needless to say, once we sold that house, we were hooked on real estate and knew just how much it could change our lives.

The only tricky thing about it is that it is often hard to take the leap of faith and just do it, even when you know all the perks. I get it! But I will add that it has been worth it every time, even with some headaches along the way. Real estate investing, including short term rentals, is all about the long game.

So, what did we do with our nest egg when we moved back to the Pacific Northwest? We moved into my in-laws' garage apartment to continue saving money while my husband started his career and I relaunched my real estate sales business. In the meantime, we still had the investment bug and were lucky enough to do some joint investments with my father-in-law in the land space. As I fondly call it, land flipping, which also turned me into the local "land expert." Between our Chicago home sale and some home runs with land, we had enough for our next property purchase.

At this point, you may be thinking, "Okay, Paige, let's get to the short term rental information." Why am I going down such a rabbit hole in our story and our primary home? Well, this all ties into our success in the short term rental space. Stick with me.

Our next purchase was for our primary residence back in our hometown, which turned into a full-blown project. Thanks to the garage life, we were able to bankroll the renovations from our nest egg and buy a home that was very manageable for us financially. My parents always taught me to live beneath my means, especially when it came to my actual home and hard expenses so that I could spend money on experiences, travel, and, in our case, real estate investments.

In the meantime, we were spending a lot of time down at the family cabin on the Washington coast. It is a deep-rooted tradition in

Chapter 2: So, Why Learn From Me?

my husband's family and my family grew to love it just as much as his did. So, with me being in real estate, during every trip down there, we toured some properties to see what was available. We probably toured properties for two years before we pulled the trigger on our first rental. Finally, when the time was right and after hours of educating myself, I said, "Well, here goes nothing!" We closed on our first short term rental in January 2021 and Anchor14 was born.

Anchor14 was our first short term rental investment. It was bought as a light renovation project that ended up being a full-blown cosmetic upgrade that included the kitchen cabinets, counters, floors, vanities, and more. It was our constant focus and took my husband nearly every weekend for six months to complete. In the meantime, we also found out we were expecting our first baby! With Amelia on the way, I became significantly less helpful in the manual labor department. Divine timing is a funny thing. While I spent more time on the couch than in the construction zone, I had time to prepare for the next phase of outfitting the house, making lists, and understanding the platforms on which I would be listing the rental. Keep in mind, aside from learning as much as I could from podcasts, I was really just shooting from the hip on how this was all going to turn out. I am a super planner but I also like to know my expected outcome and I really had no idea how any of this was going to go. So, this is your reminder, you won't know the result or exactly how to do it, but you will figure it out along the way and it will be worth it!

We launched the first week in July and, with no expectations going into it, I was blown away that reservation notification after reservation notification kept rolling in hour after hour and day after day until the rest of our summer was completely booked out. This was our HOLY SHIT moment. Like, not only did we make it to the launch after a long six months of sweat equity, but it is actually getting booked!! Yahoo!! It turned out that my somewhat guess of a method was working! Thank you, residential real estate sales, for the leg up in processes and the short term rental boom due to the pandemic.

I mention the boom because our numbers that first year were outstanding. Some of that had to do with my process and our product, but it also had to do with the state of the world and people's desire to get out and travel while being distanced from other people. The hotel industry was tanking, but the vacation rental market was flourishing. So, a little bit of divine timing and our first rental continues to be a fruitful investment to this day. I think it is worth mentioning that part of our experience included a lot of initial success because of the world we were living in at the time. Even after the pandemic had come and gone, people now prefer renting private homes rather than hotel rooms. In 2021, that was the first time that many people experienced a stay at an Airbnb listing instead of a hotel. It broadened the demographic and pool of vacationers to those who had previously only ever stayed in hotels, which expanded the vacation rental market drastically and brought it here to stay.

So, fast forward to the Spring of 2022. We had just had our lives turned upside down a few months prior with the arrival of our daughter and the very unexpected loss of my father. The world was a weird place and I was back to work helping people buy and sell real estate. Anchor14 was doing well, but we had this calling to spend more time east of the mountains in Washington. I set us up on a property search, as I often do, to keep an eye on various markets. There was a specific area that we were pretty interested in because of the outdoor attractions and its well-known golf course.

Initially, we were just looking at raw land to buy, but we found this community that had lots of land and only a couple of houses for sale.

After watching those listings, we finally decided that we should check it out to really see what this neighborhood was all about. We ended up driving over to check them out on not much more than a whim and fell in love. By the end of the day, over a lovely dinner at the local winery with our four-month-old baby, I was writing up an offer for a home with a spectacular view near all the outdoor adventures we were looking for and up the road from the popular golf course. We closed a few weeks later and Vista Ridge, our second short term rental, was born.

We ended up buying Vista Ridge as a furnished home. Since it was only a year old, we basically purchased a brand-new construction. This time around, we didn't have much sweat equity, aside from outfitting it the way that I thought it should be and changing out some light fixtures. Since this property was in somewhat of a foreign market for us, we hired a management company to handle the day-to-day details, reservations, and so on. That relationship was short-lived because I ended up taking over and self-managing. As it turned out, self-management is the way that I prefer to run our rentals.

Our third short term rental was unplanned. Normally, I wouldn't recommend that approach but, in this case, it was next door to our OG rental so we had insider information about the location, demand, and market. It was a no-brainer aside from figuring out how to pay for it. After some deliberating, we came up with a purchase plan and were able to make our dream of owning the house next door a reality. We named this home Lighthouse13 and it was the house that I based a lot of my decisions for the build-out and pricing of Anchor14. Since we were next door nearly every weekend for six months and Lighthouse13 was already a vacation rental, we became very familiar with rental demand, the type of people who were staying, how long they were staying, and the occasion for their stay. I could also watch the pricing and reviews online, so when Lighthouse13 came up for sale two years later, we jumped on it. It also made sense to pull the trigger on short notice since we already had our infrastructure with our vendors and systems in that market and had been financially preparing for our next purchase.

At the time of writing this book, we have three successful short term rentals that I personally manage. I have also helped others buy their own short term rentals, guided them through the launch process, and provided all of my tips on how to manage the listing, staff, and guests. I have curated systems to buy, outfit, launch, and manage short term rentals. I have made mistakes, I have learned as I have gone, and I have a whole host of knowledge to share with you as I encourage you to take the leap into the short term rental investing space. I wanted to write this book when I was only three vacation rentals in because I still remember what it was like to start, to be new, and to take the scary leap of faith into this investing niche. I am not that much farther ahead of you, but I have so much to pour into you.

I am writing to encourage the person who wants more for themselves, their future, and their families and wants to obtain those goals through real estate and, more specifically, through short term rental investments. The way that I do things is not the end all be all, but it sure does work. I will be walking you through how I analyze markets and properties to identify a good investment. You will learn my philosophies on furnishing your rental and where to buy things. I will show you how to properly launch your listings into the world in a way to gain the traction that you need to succeed. You will benefit from my management mistakes and learn how to avoid the errors that I have made. I will give you a very in-depth look into what it takes to be a short term rental investor and host. Since the time I was 22 years old, I have been dedicated and passionate about real estate in all its many facets. My knowledge is vast and detailed from having many different experiences for over a decade of studying and actively participating in the real estate market. You won't find a more transparent or tactical guide to have on your side as you embark on your short term rental journey. So, come along with me and let's get your first investment underway!

Chapter 3:
Here Is How It Will Work

I have organized this book into three phases—buy, launch, and manage. I know that my system works. However, full disclosure, my way of buying, launching, and managing short term rentals is going to be different from the methods used by other "gurus" in the investment education space. This book is going to be a very tactical guide on how I have successfully done it.

The buying section of the book will cover all you need to know about how to identify your market, what to look for in the property you will ultimately buy, how to structure your business plan, and how to put together your purchase terms. When it comes to becoming a short term rental investor, you will need to do your initial research about the market, what types of properties are there, what the local rules and regulations are, how much rent can be expected, and what properties can be found in your desired area cost.

Once you have all of that information, you will look into the type of property that you want to purchase whether it is a condo or a home, its condition, location, necessary amenities, and how much renovation is needed. After you have a strong foothold on the market information and what you will be looking to purchase, then you can put together your business plan and consider the amount of reserves you will need to budget accordingly. Now that you know what you are buying and how much money you will need, then I will walk you through how to structure the deal. Given my background as a residential real estate Agent, I love the art of the deal and want to share a little bit about how we have structured our purchases so far. From there, we will segue into the launch process!

In the launch section, you will learn the process of getting your rental ready for guests and how to advertise your listing. This part of the process is equal parts art and science and I will walk you through how to cast your vision, define your role, hire team members, outfit the space, and get the rental live on public platforms. This is where you will find a lot of value in the process that we have put into place.

From what I have noticed, many people feel that outfitting the space is going to be the most fun, and it is, but there are also a lot of considerations that need to be made because it is much more than just pretty furnishings and paint. The way that you set up your short term rental will determine how successful your return on investment is and how easy or challenging the property will be for you or someone else to manage.

The launch chapter will also help you define your role going forward and hire your team, both of which will dictate which way you go with the management of the property. I will go through how I get my listings ready for the world to view to ensure that you get the most traction possible in the shortest amount of time. You won't want to miss the details of my launch formula.

Lastly, I will cover everything that you need to know regarding management. It will soon be clear to you that I fully believe in self-management, and I have built out systems that make this possible for nearly anyone. I am a busy person and always adding more to my plate, so

Chapter 3: Here Is How It Will Work

if I can do it, then so can you. I will discuss the difference between self-management and hiring a management company but, ultimately, I will go through how to be able to self-manage even if you are hundreds of miles away. From security systems to the booking calendar, I go through how to hit the Superhost or Premier Host status time and time again, so you won't want to miss this section of tactical information.

I am writing this book early on in our short term rental empire-building process because I want to share our successes and pro tips as a result of the failures that we have experienced with people who want to start in this investment class but don't have a tactical guide to follow or a mentor in the STR space. I could have waited until we grew to fifteen or twenty units, but I think it honestly feels more attainable to learn from someone who isn't that much farther ahead of you in your investing journey. Sure, I have a lot of experience in the real estate industry, so I will show you exactly how we went from zero to three short term rentals in two years, how we hit those coveted platform awards every time, and how I continue to successfully manage our vendors and guests.

The only difference between me and anyone wanting to become a STR investor is that I took the leap. I did it. I decided that this was the vehicle in real estate investing that I wanted to utilize and I did my best to learn as much as I could. But, when it comes down to it, you have to start before you are ready. Take the first step forward by starting to look at markets, touring some properties, getting a pre-approval, determining how much you can afford, calculating what type of cash flow is possible, figuring out who you know in that area, and meeting people to be your future vendors. Get out there and get started.

Let's get you ready to buy, launch, and manage your very own short term rental!

Part 1:
Let's Buy This Thing

Chapter 4:
How To Choose Your Market

When you embark on the journey to become a short term rental owner and host, you will first need to do some research to understand the area. The key to a successful short term rental is to make sure you have a beat on the market that you are buying in so that you can curate your purchase to fit the needs of your future guests while meeting your financial goals and resources. Aside from nailing down what type of property you should be providing to the rental market, it will also help you determine how financially prepared you need to be and what type of property you will be shopping for. To fully understand the market you are thinking about buying in, you will want to be aware of the local economics, attractions, seasonality, and regulations. You will need to look at the currently available listings to determine your future competition, the rates, and how you can be one of the best rentals that the market offers.

Since you are taking the time to read this book, I am guessing that becoming an STR owner or host is something that you have considered for some time. Maybe you even have a market picked out and you are like, "YES, I would LOVE to own a home here and make it a super dreamy vacation rental!" So, when you imagine that being your life, where is that rental located? Maybe you go on vacation annually and you are like, "It would be a lifelong dream to own a property here." Okay, great. Now that you are imagining that, let's go through the rest of this chapter with your special location in mind.

The success of your short term rental will absolutely depend on the location, location, location and the market that you choose to purchase in. Now, I am not saying that you need to pick one of the top tourist destinations like San Diego, Palm Springs, Miami, Destin, Nashville, etc. I personally chose a market that is a tourist town, but one that is on a much smaller scale and not necessarily known outside of the state. The size of the market will dictate the buy-in purchase threshold, otherwise known as the price point, that you can expect when buying there. That being said, you want to choose a market that has attractions, things to do, and a reason for people to be there. Why do people go there? Would you want to go there? If so, what would you do? Go through an exercise of planning a trip itinerary. If you were going there with friends for the weekend, what would your days look like? What activities would you do? What would you pack? Where would you eat? All of these questions will not only inform where you buy but also impact what you buy and how you outfit the property.

I think that the easiest way to choose a market is to think of the places that you like to visit, vacation, escape to, or travel to for work. Maybe you need to do some more market research by going on some weekend trips or checking out the real estate in the area on your next work trip. If you are traveling there for work or leisure, then it is likely that other people are too! This also plays into how close to home you want your short term rental to be.

The other advantage to choosing a market that you like to visit or go to for work is that you are already the area expert. You understand it, which means that your personal experience will elevate your new short term rental into a better place for guests to visit because you know who your ideal guest is—and they are likely similar to you and share your interests or needs.

If it is a place you escape to with one local bar and restaurant, then you will know what you need to outfit the property with for it to be comfortable for guests who will be hunkering down and maybe having "one night out" at the local haunt. You will need to make sure your kitchen is well stocked with cooking and baking necessities and your Guest Guide should inform your guests about the amenities that you have provided for them to enjoy their "staycation" in your home. If your location is a place where professionals travel for work, then you will outfit your space with high-speed internet, clean and minimalist furnishings, and amenities that they will appreciate during their business trip. Think of a list of things that they can order and a list of rideshare options. Does your town have Uber or Lyft, or both? If it has neither, how should they catch a ride to and from their destination? Picking the location informs your type of guest, which in turn informs the way you approach your amenities list.

Before you get too far down the research path, you will also want to deep dive into what local regulations are in place for short term rentals. With all good things, as soon as they hit a certain level of popularity or become an industry disruptor, restrictions quickly follow. (I am looking at you, Uber!) In many cities and locations across the United States, there have been stifling restrictions against short term rental owners and hosts.

I know that when we started with our first rental in 2020, the rules were more lax than they are today after the STR boom, thanks to the Pandemic. The best thing to do is to call and talk to the governing office to hear straight from them what the process is. In both of our markets, the local officials were very helpful and friendly in getting us through the process. I get the feeling that they like the owners who follow the rules!

My husband and I chose our initial rental market based on the fact that it was in a relatively affordable market, had tourism as a main draw, and we are intimately familiar with it. Plus, the permit process was simple with reasonable regulations. We chose a coastal town in Washington state because it was a place that my husband's family had been going to since the 1920s. His great-grandparents built the cabin across from the local hardware store that we still visit to this day. Since Jeff grew up going there along with the generations before him, he is an expert on the ebbs and flows of the market and what continues to draw people to come visit, year after year and season after season.

Our market is also exactly two hours from our main home, which made our first purchase manageable over the six-month period that we were renovating it. For us, proximity, especially for our first one, was a priority. We have found that having a property within two hours of our home is the most convenient. That way, when we need to go for some quick repairs or to drop off supplies, we can either go for the day or for just one night without it being too difficult.

If you are going to be self-managing, you will want to think about the distance of the property from your primary residence or where you currently live. Some people will want to be in the same town, others will be comfortable being within a couple of hours, and still others will be just fine being states away. There is no right answer to this one, but it is something that you will want to think about. Can you drive there in a day? Does driving distance matter and, if so, why? How about flying distance? Are you comfortable and able to hop on a flight if you need to? All of these things will be determined by your trust level with your "boots on the ground" team that you hire, which I will cover later on. However, most of the time, you have a gut feeling about what your comfort level will be, especially for your first rental. I am here to tell you that any distance is doable; it just depends on you, your lifestyle, and your team.

Chapter 4: How To Choose Your Market

Since it was already a place that we were visiting multiple times a year to go to the family cabin, we started touring properties every time we were in Grayland so we could familiarize ourselves with the real estate market, pricing, and common maintenance and repair items for the area. PS. It's a thing to have varying property concerns from region to region. Certain issues will arise time and time again with homes based on the location, climate, etc. In our case, it is common for homes in our area to have post and pier or block foundations, so when we found the house that would become our first short term rental, we were pretty excited that it had a poured concrete foundation with a basement. However, we weren't shying away from the post and pier or block foundations when we were shopping since that just comes with the territory. It is also a very wet climate so pooling or standing water around foundations is very common. For comparison, homes where we primarily reside would practically be condemned for having considerable amounts of standing water near the foundation.

Every market, climate, and area will have certain sticking points. I learned that when I went from selling real estate in Western Washington to the Chicago suburbs in Illinois—we do not have the same problems and concerns but homes still all function the same way, which is a great piece of perspective to have when you are house shopping and reviewing an inspection report. There are also solutions to almost every problem or "issue," so you just need to know what the solution options are and how much they will cost.

The next things you want to consider are the growth of popularity and population, stability of the market, and trajectory for tourism. Is this a town that is continuing to grow? Is it a ghost town? Is it declining in popularity? If so, why? Where do you see the future of the area? Is there anything that will cause the town to grow in population and popularity over the next decade? What type of industries are there? What supports the local economy?

All of these things will impact your occupancy rate and, more importantly, they will impact your appreciation. At the end of the day, you are likely getting into short term rentals to provide a brighter financial future for yourself, so you will want to keep appreciation at the forefront of your mind when deciding where to buy. Having an asset appreciate over time is part of the secret sauce of what makes owning a STR magical.

In our case, people are visiting our town to go to the ocean, visit the beach, enjoy a slower-paced lifestyle for a few days, escape the city, go fishing, and go crabbing or clam digging. Our town is a commercial fishing town that attracts a lot of tourism, which is a staple in bringing people to the coast. We found that this creates stability for the occupancy of our home. Back in 2019 when we started shopping religiously on our trips, we also knew that there were rumblings of a golf course being built, which would provide a good amount of growth in the area. Not only would it be a public golf course, but it was similar to the ever-popular Bandon Dunes on the Oregon coast because it was built by the same well-known designer. We knew that we couldn't bank on this coming to fruition, but it made the case for this location even stronger.

When you are looking into the potential restrictions, regulations, or permits for short term rentals in your desired market, you will want to first do some Googling. There are often articles published about any existing or future restrictions on the horizon. You will also want to check with the city council or the county office to see what is currently in place or potentially coming down the pipe. If you find a market without restrictions, you are lucky! If you have your eyes set on a larger market like Palm Springs, then you will have a tougher time breaking into that market as a STR owner. Towns that have been dealing with short term rentals for a long time have had more time to implement restrictions and figure out the actual impact on that city so they should be pretty clear. If you buy in a place that is new to having a bustling STR market, then you will likely either be in the phase of being Grandfathered in with fewer restrictions or be experiencing the evolution of their restrictions.

In our case, we got into our initial rental market when the permitting process was pretty simple. Even between the times that we bought our first and our second, the process had gotten a bit more regulated. I will advise you to keep up with these ever-changing processes and requirements. You want the controlling authorities to be your friend, not your foe. They do, after all, determine whether your permit is approved or not!

Each city or town is going to handle things differently but across the two markets where we own and operate our rentals, there are a few similarities. First of all, they all cost money. You will be on the hook for a permit fee. In one town, it is a one-time fee; in the other, it is an annual fee. We are also required to have smoke detectors, carbon monoxide detectors, fire extinguishers, emergency contacts, and floor plans. In our coastal rentals, we also needed to provide an evacuation route in the event of a tsunami. In our eastern Washington property, we needed to provide evacuation information in the event of a wildfire. I have found that the people at the city or the county levels are very helpful in explaining what is needed. Generally, they have an online application that maps out what you will need to provide to get an approved permit. It makes for a much smoother process if you follow the instructions and turn in everything that they need all at the same time.

Here are some examples of restrictions and permitting processes between the areas where we have our rentals:

+ Annual permit and fee
+ Annual well test with satisfactory results
+ Only one short term rental per household
+ Initial permit and fee
+ On-site inspection before approval
+ Weekly garbage service
+ Quarterly tourism reporting and taxation

For one of our properties, we are inside of a community that is governed by a homeowner's association so we have to comply with their rules and restrictions as well. That is a story for another book but keep in mind when you are shopping whether or not the property is controlled by community restrictions. In our case, we pay an additional annual fee to our homeowner's association in addition to our annual dues just because we rent our home out. They also enacted a new rule that tenants cannot use the community amenities such as the pool and clubhouse.

As you can see, things from town to town and county to county will differ, so your best resource is to go to the source and ask what they require. The one thing you can never predict is what the future holds, but it is a good idea to get a beat on what conversations are happening in the community surrounding short term rentals. Some places will be much more friendly about it than others.

During your research phase, you will not only be looking at the market itself but also at what type of properties are available, either for sale or for rent. This research phase is far-reaching so you will want to look at as much of the demographics as possible.

Now that you have your location in mind and you have gotten the regulations part out of the way, you will want to imagine that you are going to stay in this town yourself. What types of activities would you be doing? What attractions would you be visiting? Where would you be staying? What would make your stay here better? What location is ideal and what is the best location without being the most expensive? How many people would be traveling and what would be their situation? Would they travel solo? With couples? Groups? Families? Friends? Bachelor/ette destination? Romantic getaway? Are they outdoor enthusiasts? If it is a work hub, your space would be geared toward professionals. What would they need to make their stay more enjoyable?

When we chose our first market to invest in, we understood the local demographics, what it had to offer, why people were going there, and what type of seasonality it had. We also chose a market that wasn't super expensive or fancy. That meant the bar was pretty low in terms of competition and we were confident with my background in real estate sales and marketing that we could provide a superior product. We also researched the types of listings that were available and determined which ones were renting the most, got the highest rental rates, and had the most popular locations and amenities.

In our case, we figured out that there really weren't many options for larger groups of people to stay, so we made it our mission to build out a space that could sleep 10 people comfortably. I am not talking about accommodating extra people with air mattresses and sleeper sofas. The house that we bought is a two-bedroom, so we created a "third" bedroom by building out a custom bunk bed that provided a queen mattress on the bottom with twin beds on top. It was crafted in such a way that the top and bottom beds were perpendicular to one another so it was easy for an adult to get in and out of the bottom bunk. We wanted to build something that, if we were to be the ones sleeping in the bunk area, we wouldn't feel slighted. We also had a double-sided bookshelf installed to create privacy and storage between the two bottom bunks, which also includes remote-controlled lights. These features didn't cost much but those thoughtful attention-to-detail additions absolutely made an impact on our guest experience.

As I mentioned, one of the ways we determined what we were shopping for in our first rental was by looking at the current short term rental offerings. This sort of recon is something I am very familiar with as a realtor, so I had no problem diving right in. My trick for those of you who aren't used to such sleuthing is to start scrolling through the entire market first. If you have already picked a town or location that piques your interest, then pull up the available listings on Airbnb and VRBO. There are other websites or apps you can check out, but in my experience these two are the most widely used. Then dive in and start perusing what's available, how they are presented on the app, what sort of amenities they have, what price ranges they are offered at, and how many there are. All of these things will determine what you will be shopping for based on demand and market standards.

When you are looking at these listings, keep in mind the amount of available listings. How many of those listings would you personally be interested in renting? Are you noticing any trends in terms of amenities, style of spaces, and number of people that the listings can accommodate? How competitive are the listings in your target market? Are there tons of listings? Are they well-appointed? Do they look great from the online listing? How do the nightly rates stack up to what home prices are in the area?

For example, when we were buying our first rental, we were looking at homes for no more than $350,000. Our payment would be around $1,500 a month and I was banking on an average of 8 nights per month that would be booked at a rate of $300 a night. This would likely be a conservative scenario—and it was—and would well exceed our monthly expenses. I like to use the calculation metric of eight nights booked per month because it should be more than that in a popular and stable vacation destination so your ultimate performance should be better than that on average. If the numbers work with only eight nights a month booked, then it makes good sense to go for it. You could probably use ten to twelve nights a month depending on the popularity of the market, but I like to play it safe when I am analyzing a deal. The good news is that it made sense to buy these properties with a monthly occupancy of eight and these homes hit or exceed that annual need in their peak seasons alone. Don't worry, I will talk more about numbers shortly.

With all of this research under your belt, you now have an idea of what you would potentially be shopping for, so head on over to Zillow or whatever your favorite public real estate platform is and look at available homes for sale. Seeing what is available for sale will bring your research full circle and allow you to decipher the correlation between purchase price and rental price. After years of being in residential real estate sales, I can venture a guess that you probably have a price-point in mind when it comes to your purchase. Seeing the availability of properties, their prices, and what they will potentially rent for will give you a clear direction about whether or not this market will work for you or if you need to adjust your expectations, bring in a partner, or consider a different market.

Chapter 5:
What To Buy

Now that you know the lay of the land in your desired market, let's dive into what you are really going to be shopping for. There are many different types of properties and their availability will be more or less common depending on the location. If you read or listen to anything relating to real estate, you will hear certain name classifications such as single family, condo, duplex, townhouse, and so on. What in the world do all of these things mean and what makes for the best short term rentals? That answer isn't cut and dry, but I am going to lay out your options so you know which option will likely be the best fit for you. All property types have different levels of maintenance, responsibilities, and fees that you may not be thinking about when you are embarking on this journey. I am here to uncover the mysterious lingo that real estate professionals use as if it's common knowledge.

Option 1: Single Family Property

Let's start with the term "single family." This refers to a stand alone, one-residential unit. When you picture the quintessential "I bought a house!" photo, you think of an individual, family, or a couple standing on the porch in front of a one or two story home with a yard and maybe even a picket fence. This is a single family home. Picture suburbia with all the homes that sprawl for miles, have sidewalk-lined neighborhoods, and are on cul-de-sacs. Although those things are not all requirements, that is the easiest way to identify a single family home.

When it comes to a single family home, you are responsible for all of the maintenance of the home and the yard unless your neighborhood is controlled by a homeowners association (HOA) that includes yard maintenance in their fee. However, in the context of short term rentals, you likely won't choose a neighborhood with a vast HOA because they also likely include restrictions regarding rentals, especially those of the short term variety.

All three homes that my husband and I currently have as short term rentals are single family homes. We personally like that model over other types of properties. The pros to having a single family home as a short term rental is that the structure stands alone. You don't share any walls with neighbors, which will likely keep complaints about short term guests at bay. We also like to be able to offer our guests a yard of some sort since all of our rentals are kid and pet friendly. By having a single family home, we can also offer more exterior amenities like a bonfire pit, outdoor seating, yard space for kids, hot tubs, and extra parking spaces. We also always think about what type of property we would rent since we are the type of family that is most comfortable in a single family home especially when we are with extended family or friends.

Option 2: Condominiums

The next property type you may be considering is a condo. When people think of a condo, they think of an apartment that you own instead of rent, but, in actuality, any property type can be a condo. The term "condominium" refers to owning the airspace within the unit that one owns with non-exclusive ownership of the shared amenities. So, when you think of a traditional condominium, you are correct to think of an apartment building where everyone owns their unit since they do, but all owners also have a shared interest in the joint amenities such as the building itself, common areas of a business center or gym, and exterior spaces like the parking lots and garages.

When you own a condo, you are not the sole person responsible for when the roof or siding needs to be replaced since the whole complex will share in that expense. At first glance, that may sound like great news, but you also have to realize that the cost of replacing a roof or siding may be much larger than a standard home and may come with commercial replacement costs. The way those expenses get paid is through special assessments, which are levied when a large project is needed for the complex and they are due on top of your monthly homeowner association dues. Keep in mind that I am bringing up the topic of an HOA again, which means you will need to make sure that the condo complex allows rentals, let alone short term rentals, before you get too far along with your interest level.

The pros to pursuing a condominium purchase for a short term rental is if you are in a more expensive market because condos tend to be less expensive. Or they can initially appear that way before factoring in the monthly dues. Condos are wonderful for people who are not interested in either doing maintenance themselves or paying for it. Since you only have to worry about the fixtures and finishes inside your unit, you potentially will have far fewer maintenance costs, which should be factored into your calculations.

As long as short term rentals are allowed in your prospective condo complex, then you can also benefit from the fact that the complex generally has shared amenities that your guests will be able to enjoy, such as a pool, fitness center, dedicated parking, or security. Condos also tend to be located centrally to nearby attractions, restaurants, and amenities. In short, they can be an automatic "no" for short term rental investors due to restrictions, but they can be a great option for your first rental purchase instead of taking on a whole house with all of its maintenance costs and other responsibilities.

Option 3: Duplex

Duplexes are most often talked about in relation to long term rentals, but they can make wonderful short term rentals. "Du" means "two," so a duplex is a structure that houses two units. They often are constructed in a way that the two units share one wall or are joined by the garage walls to ensure less noise transfers between households. However, many homes have been converted from single family homes to duplexes, which happens most often in places with older homes. Duplexes tend to be close to area attractions, amenities, or city centers and often have a yard of some sort for each unit or a shared yard space giving your guests added amenities and space.

When it comes to these conversions, you want to make sure they were done properly and are supplying each unit with the appropriate power and water that they will need to function safely. This is where your home inspection will come in handy to uncover any of those potential hazards. If you just buy a duplex that was constructed to be that way from the start, however, you will have two units ready to rent on any lease term that you desire.

What I love most about duplexes is their flexibility. I have clients that bought duplexes where they furnish and short term rent out one side while they mid term (30 days to six-month terms) the other side. This strategy creates stability while also taking advantage of the higher rent rates that both short and mid term rentals bring. These properties also offer you the easiest exit strategies in the event that your short term rental dreams don't work for whatever reason, whether because you realize that you hate the short turnovers and management aspects or because the market isn't as favorable for short term rentals. Whatever the reason may be, you can easily transition to mid term rentals or long term rentals, having the power to pivot to Plans B or C without much hassle.

Option 4: Townhouse

A townhouse is most often a home that is tall and consists of 2 or 3 floors. They share similar traits to a duplex or condo given that you likely share at least one wall with a neighboring unit, there is likely to be an association that dictates fees and rules, and you may either have shared or individual outdoor space. Again, the advantages of townhomes are that they require less yard maintenance and share in the exterior maintenance and replacement costs. They tend to be in smaller blocks of units, so the replacement costs should be similar to a single family home. You just want to keep your ideal guest in mind because not everyone will be able to rent a place with two or three flights of stairs.

You will also want to reference the type of properties that Airbnb often favors or already has a classification for. At the top of the app, you will notice that they have a search function where you can browse by type of property—cabin, yurt, boat, camping, luxury, lakefront, tiny, beachfront, amazing views, and many more. Can you purchase a property that fits one of these categories and lean into that theme?

Think back to when you were scrolling on Zillow. What types of properties were most prevalent? What about when you were scrolling through Airbnb? Is there a certain property type that is most often offered for rent? What properties were performing the best? What amenities and attributes did they have? Following this market research process will narrow down your search so you become crystal clear on what you should be purchasing to get the best return on your short term rental investment.

Once you have determined what type of property you will be shopping for, then you will want to consider the condition that your future rental will be in when you purchase it. The condition will determine how quickly your launch process will go, the amount of cash reserves you need going into it, and your initial purchase price.

While you are gearing up to make this purchase, you need to think about what you are willing and able to accomplish when it comes to getting your property ready to outfit. Your options will include turnkey, cosmetic upgrades, or a full-blown renovation.

You will often hear real estate professionals talk about a home being "turnkey," especially in their marketing remarks when a home is for sale. The sentiment is that all you have to do is turn the key to the lock and the home is ready to move into. Another fan favorite that means the same thing is "move-in ready." At this point in the process, you will want to be real with yourself about what you should really be taking on. Turnkey may be the right choice for you if you are most comfortable just diving into furnishing the home instead of adding value through renovations.

An excellent option for someone who wants to add a lot of their own style to their property is to choose something that needs some cosmetic upgrades but not a complete gut or overhaul. When I say "cosmetic upgrade," I am generally referring to painting kitchen cabinets, changing out some hardware, and maybe giving the bathrooms some upgrades like lighting, mirrors, and paint. Even changing out vanities and faucets isn't too spendy as long as the flooring can be salvaged in the process.

I would not, however, classify a full kitchen renovation as a cosmetic upgrade—and I am speaking from experience! On our first short term rental property, we went from planning a cosmetic renovation—painting cabinets, changing hardware, replacing carpet, and removing popcorn ceiling—to tearing everything out of the house to the point that there was only drywall left. That was a much more expensive and time-intensive project than we originally planned. In the end, it worked out great for us but was certainly not what we set out to do. So my wisdom in hindsight is that as soon as you decide to start doing a major renovation on one part of your property, don't be surprised if it snowballs into a whole house renovation.

We ended up doing a full renovation on our first short term rental because we had intended to replace the upstairs carpeted flooring with luxury plank vinyl. As soon as we got all of the carpet out, we also removed a bank of kitchen cabinets that were blocking the view from the kitchen to the rest of the living area. We determined that the quality of the kitchen cabinets was too poor to salvage and paint, so a full-blown kitchen and living space renovation was upon us.

Once we started designing our beautiful new kitchen, it was clear that we needed to renovate the bathrooms as well. We were able to keep the existing tub, showers, and toilets but we painted the walls and installed all new bathroom flooring and vanities. It was clear to us as soon as we started the kitchen renovation that the bathrooms needed to be brought up to the same level of luxury. The beauty of our process was that my husband was the contractor on the project, so we saved on labor costs but we certainly did not save on time! My husband drove the two hours each way almost every single weekend for six months from the time we closed until it was ready to launch. We closed on the home in January and listed it on Airbnb by the first week in July.

If you don't have the financial backing, time, or resources to accomplish that type of project, then stick to your original cosmetic upgrade plan. One way to determine your game plan is to think about what you must do to make the home attractive to your ideal guests. If you determine that you must do a kitchen renovation, then you likely will need to also do bathroom renovations because having a beautiful new kitchen and dingy old bathrooms just don't flow right or deliver the quality experience that your guest will be expecting. By the time you are ripping out cabinets and putting in new ones, you will likely end up doing new floors throughout as well.

When it comes to a full renovation, you will want to get your contractor involved from the first time you visit a property, or at least by the time you determine that it is a viable option for your rental purchase. The reason is that you will need to be realistic about what can be done and what a potential budget will be. You shouldn't embark on any investment purchase without knowing what the numbers look like because it can get extremely out of balance when you decide a full renovation is the way that you want to go. When it comes to rental revenue, you especially want to factor in how much your monthly carrying costs are as well as how quickly you will be able to earn back any renovation costs.

> Refer back to the QR code for free calculators

Keep in mind that renovations are just one part of the process of getting your home listed on vacation rental platforms. For this first one, unless you have a background in producing quality construction, you may want to choose something that is on the side of move-in ready to not get you too bogged down on your journey to hosting. These properties may be more expensive and you will need to weigh that against what you would be spending in money AND time by doing renovations on a property.

I see it all the time with my buyer clients. They get hooked by a certain price and flippantly consider the upgrades or repairs that they need to do, which isn't always the best strategy. It can cost you money and time if you don't have the proper help or skills to get those things accomplished. By buying a property that is ready to start the outfitting process, you cut down your launch time significantly. The property also will likely not need many maintenance repairs in the near future, so this will give you a chance to start bringing in revenue to start saving for future needs.

Again, renovation doesn't have to mean high-end because it should reflect the market area. If anything, your renovation should reflect the theme of your rental, which is influenced by its location and competition. You need to keep in mind that you aren't renovating your forever home and that this home is not for you. Let me say that again: This home is not for you! This home is for your ideal guest who will be traveling to your market area. The fun part is that you get to choose the market, which means that you will likely have a lot in common with your ideal guests and that you will make decisions based on your own opinion. I just need to remind you that this house is not for you so that you keep any decisions that are too specific to you out of the picture.

I am a big fan of sweat equity. I am lucky enough to be married to my business partner who is extremely talented when it comes to construction and designing spaces, so we get to tackle these projects for less out-of-pocket, but we also spend a lot more of our personal time executing these renovations.

In the end, it works for us. We love that we build equity by doing things ourselves and that we know the work was done well and in the right way. This also saves us money in the long run because if something needs to be repaired, we know how it was done to begin with and are likely able to avoid having to rip things out and start from scratch later.

Quality control is a big thing for us. The sweat equity that we get in return is also part of our big-picture goal.

My biggest advice is to avoid any sweat equity projects that are outside of your realm of capability. This is not the time to give wiring and plumbing a go, but it is a great time to paint, clean, and learn from your contractor. Spending money to have things done right from the beginning will save you so much in the long run.

No matter the direction you go with a renovation or any upgrades, these things need to happen before you can start outfitting your space. You will need to build out a timeline for completion, which will also inform your projected budget and the hard carrying costs like your mortgage, utilities, and taxes while the work is getting done.

Okay, so now you have an idea of what type of condition the property should be in from a feasibility standpoint. Next, we want to consider the market nuances and how they will affect your potential renovations.

Your market will absolutely influence the level of finishes you need to have in order to be successful. Each market is going to vary in terms of the types of properties that are available, the price point for rent, and how fancy or cabin chic you will want to go. If you are buying a rental in a market that is rich in history and old homes, then you can lean into that old world charm and probably should avoid going ultra modern. If you are buying an off-grid cabin in the woods, then you will want to lean into a cabin chic aesthetic with all the modern amenities while still using furnishings that feel like you're in a cabin in the woods and not in a French chalet. If you are buying a townhouse in the middle of a hustling and bustling city, then you want to cater to décor that is more modern, sleek, and comfortable for those traveling for work or dwelling in the city. You get what I am saying. Guests in your market will be most drawn to properties that feel like they belong in that setting.

Chapter 5: What To Buy

Moving on from renovation, let's talk location, location, location. The old tried and true rule of buying real estate for the location and not for the finishes is sage advice for anyone buying their primary home and especially for those buying a rental. In all cases, real estate is an asset, and the best way to win in real estate is to buy something in a great location that will allow it to appreciate faster and fetch higher rental rates.

Depending on the market that you are buying in, you will want to consider proximity to bars, restaurants, activities, sightseeing landmarks, the beach, prized hiking trails, the river, the winery, or whatever it is that brings people to your area. You also receive bonus points if you can get within prime walking distance of these locations without breaking the bank. Or, if you are buying in a remote location, make sure that the house is reasonably accessible and has some other draw like views, trails, or purely quiet seclusion.

Once you have nailed the location, you want to determine what grand amenities will be necessary to be a huge hit with renters. When I say "grand amenities," I am talking about the big features of the property and not the little niceties like complimentary coffee, shampoo, a hair dryer, workspace, and so on—we will discuss those things later. I am talking about the amenities that will attract more renters and for higher rates. Maybe it is a must-have to have a pool, hot tub, yard, or garage. With the location, available homes, and your financial position, are those amenities going to be feasible? Are there homes for sale that already have some of those features? If not, are they something that you can easily add? How will those amenities affect your timeline, budget, and projected rent rates? When people are looking to book a vacation rental, they are driven by the features that are offered with the property.

You will need to do a lot of sleuthing on Airbnb and VRBO to determine what properties are available in your market, what the rental rates tend to be, how often they are booked, which ones have the best reviews, and why they are so desirable. Most places get the most reviews because they are eye-catching, which makes them the top pick for people traveling there. They then cement the likelihood of a good review by having a well-stocked home that is clean above all else.

You will also likely notice a trend in the properties that rent the best, the amenities that they offer, and the type of finishes that the unit has. Like with all things in business and life, don't reinvent the wheel. If certain styles are performing well, then do that. Just lean into your own version of that style. When it comes to short term rentals, you want to keep furnishing on the more minimal side so the space feels free of clutter while also having every amenity any person visiting would potentially need—within reason.

By now, I would venture to guess that your brain is churning on all the details that will set your foundation for your short term rental, things that aren't sexy. Yet, I hope this chapter has gotten you to think about things that you may not have taken into consideration before. My request is that you get real with yourself about what you are actually able and willing to do. I feel like the biggest pitfall at this stage is to embark on a renovation or build-out that is more of a pipe dream than a realistic business plan. Speaking of business plans, let's talk numbers.

Chapter 6:
The Financial Position to Succeed

This will arguably be the most boring but crucial chapter in this section of the book. Even though I know that all of this sounds very fun and exciting, it is a business. So, you must prepare to run it as one. Without a business and financial plan, you can get yourself into trouble very quickly. On the flip side, the plan doesn't need to be exhaustive or elaborate. You just need to have a clear picture of what it will take financially and on what timeline you will need to get to the finish line of launching and beyond.

When you are building out your business plan, you will need to take into consideration the following things: upfront costs, carrying costs, maintenance and repair savings, projected rental income, and occupancy rates. No matter what type of property you purchase, all of these categories will apply. When you are building out your proposal, it is really just an estimate so, as I said above, I would highly recommend overestimating how much things will cost and how long things will take, especially for your first one. You are not only paying to get your home up and running but you are also paying for your education. That may sound odd, but what I mean is that you will be learning the whole way through this first short term rental experience, which will cost you time and money. That's okay! It is expected and a part of the process.

To be honest, I didn't even realize that I had a process when I embarked on my first vacation rental but once we bought our second and our third rentals, I had determined that I had this down to a functional science. Truth be told, we did not have a business plan or real budget for the first rental. Yikes! We basically just bankrolled it as needed as we went. I would never recommend that route, but thankfully it all worked out. Part of that was also because of the timing of the market. We bought in January of 2021 and the vacation rental market was BOOMING as the pandemic continued. So, in that regard, I would say we experienced beginners' luck if you will. I am very glad, however, to know that you will not be starting this journey blindly.

When it comes to upfront costs, I am referring to the costs of actually purchasing the property. I will discuss these things in detail in a future chapter but, for quick reference, I am talking about the down payment, closing costs, inspections, initial renovation, and buildout costs. From there, you need to consider your carrying costs—monthly mortgage, utilities, taxes, HOA fee (if applicable), insurance, snow removal, pool and hot tub care, lawn service, etc. You will also want to be prepared with a savings amount for repairs and maintenance. Things will break or need attention and you will need to be financially prepared. Then, of course, you need to project your rental rates and occupancy, which will result in your expected monthly revenue.

Your projected monthly revenue is going to dictate your business plan. You have to know what you can expect to have coming in to be able to budget properly. There is no business if you can't afford to keep the doors open. My favorite way to handle a business plan is to start with the end in mind and then work backward from there. If you project a well-producing rental in your market will be able to bring in $5,000 a month in rental revenue on average and some months will be double or triple that, then you can base your monthly expense allowance on those numbers. Your expense allowance will then inform your monthly mortgage amount, which will in turn inform your purchase price or amount you can finance versus having to put down in cash. You can get estimates from local utility companies on their costs so you can build that into your estimate as well. Then make sure to factor in seasonal services such as lawn service or snow plowing.

I find that if you are already a homeowner, you should just sit down and write down every housing or property expense you have had in the last few years. Then make sure to take into account the things that you need to have fixed or replaced at your house that you haven't because you can live without it, things that won't fly in short term rental land. Next, consider the service you need to pay for maintenance if you do not do them yourself like cleaning your gutters and windows, pressure washing the patio or deck, seasonal yard overhaul, servicing the furnace and hot water heater, etc. Not all of these things will necessarily come into play, but it is better to be prepared.

Now that you are thinking about all of those details, let me run you through a good old hypothetical scenario. I will talk about funding your purchase in the following chapter, but for the sake of painting a picture I will run you through an example of getting your listing ready to go and what financial bandwidth may look like.

With a purchase price of $325,000 and a conventional loan, you need to put 25% down for the best rates, which would come to $81,250. Don't forget to add on the closing cost fees, which are $8,000. Inspection costs are another $750. So, your cash out of pocket to start is $90,000.00.

+ Down payment: $81,250
+ Closing Costs: $8,000
+ Inspection $750
+ Cash out of pocket to purchase: $90,000

Now, let's say you are planning to do a partial renovation that you project to cost you $18,000 for some new carpet, paint, trim, and hardware, all of which you will hire a contractor for. Your initial cash output at this point is $108,000. That partial renovation is expected to take three weeks to complete. The good news is that your first monthly payment isn't due for six weeks!

While you're waiting on the contractor, you are sourcing all of your furnishings, housewares, and interior amenities, which you expect to cost $10,000. As soon as your renovation projects are complete, you can go ahead and do the installation of the furnishings and get the house outfitted. You expect the installation to take five days to get it just how you want it and you hire a friend to help you move things into the home and get organized, which costs you $1,000 in labor. You also saved money by cleaning the home yourself. We're now up to $119,000 in cash output.

+ Cash out of pocket to purchase: $90,000
+ Renovations: $18,000
+ Furnishing: $10,000
+ Hired help: $1,000
+ Total cash output at this point: $119,000

The house is now photo ready! So, you pay a professional photographer to come out and do photos, video, and drone to capture the home in its best light possible. Your photographer charges $1,200. You are now four weeks past your closing date, so your mortgage payment isn't due for another two weeks. Cash output: $120,200.

Let's do a soft launch! Offer a super discounted stay to your family and friends for one weekend, which will cover the cleaning fee to run through your processes and work out any kinks.

Chapter 6: The Financial Position to Succeed

Okay, now you are ready to go live on Airbnb! You set your rates to ensure that you will be the best option for the best price and so you get your first booking for the following weekend. That brings in enough rent to cover a third of your upcoming mortgage payment.

Your $1,960 mortgage payment gets made, but you only had to individually fund $1,307. So your current out-of-pocket is $121,507.

+ Total cash output to gear up: $119,000
+ Professional photos: $1,200
+ First booking payment: +$653
+ Remaining mortgage cost: $1307
+ ALL IN TOTAL CASH USED: $121,507

Now you are off to the races with bookings and can cover all the carrying costs, plus receive an average of $3,000 in excess revenue per month.

So, after walking through that scenario, is that plan feasible for you financially? What if that is the best case scenario? How much longer could you make the monthly payments without rental income covering the costs? How fast would you need to pay back your initial investment of $121,507?

With this breakdown, does that work for your financial goals and plan? How long will it take you to get your investment back? Maybe you need to get those funds back quickly. What needs to change? Or maybe you need to realistically admit that you can't input that much cash upfront? Don't forget the other benefits of owning a short term rental. If you have other real estate holdings, or plan to, this is just one piece of your investment puzzle. Keep in mind that there are tax benefits. If you are still working a day job, then this investment will allow you to offset some of the income if you plan it right. So, as much of this is a numbers game to be a successful rental, it should also be part of your tax strategy, wealth-building roadmap, and retirement plan. Work with a tax professional to figure out what will work best for your personal situation and ultimate goals.

As I mentioned previously, my rule of thumb for the financials is to double your estimated costs and timelines. When we are planning, we tend to get excited about the possibilities and often are too optimistic about the numbers. You will be so much happier and more financially secure if you are very conservative during your underwriting process. The best practice is to set aside six months of carrying costs in the event that occupancy is way down or you have a major repair that keeps you from renting the property. The cost to outfit the property will vary, and I will discuss that more later, but generally $10,000 to $12,000 for a 2,000 sq foot home can be expected for midrange furnishings. Then, once you do start renting the property, do not spend any of the income on anything aside from necessities for at least the first two years. This should give you a good financial foundation for that property.

This underwriting process will be the backbone of your investing success. When it comes to entrepreneurship, we tend to get so wrapped up in all the possibilities that we sometimes aren't realistic with the numbers. This may be the time for you to tap into a partner, mentor, or anyone with an outside perspective that is perhaps more realistic and will be very helpful in keeping you grounded. On the flip side, maybe you are the more cautious, pessimistic one, so you actually need someone to walk through the numbers with you to make sure you aren't passing on a good deal just because you are only thinking of the worst-case scenario. You need to land somewhere in the middle between possibility and worst-case scenario. It is likely that if you have a partner in this endeavor that they have a different set of skills than you, which will serve you well in this part of the journey. It is good to collaborate and bounce ideas off of someone else to make sure your numbers are making sense; however, the big thing will be to make sure you look at the data and what is currently available in your market. Just like in real estate sales, it is a beauty pageant. You need to have the best-looking rental with good amenities for the best price in order to achieve a thriving occupancy rate.

Chapter 7:
The Deal

Okay! Now you are ready to move from window shopping online towards actively shopping and making an offer. In this chapter, I will cover everything from the financing options available to how the actual buying process is going to go. Being an Agent myself, I have found that many people aren't even aware of their financing options, and they certainly don't know what to expect in the buying process once they decide that this is the right investment for them. So, I am here to give you insight into both monumental pieces of this experience.

Your Options

So, the biggest question is, how am I going to afford to buy my short term rental? Well, that's a great question! And there are many answers, from conventional financing loans and HELOCs to commercial lending, private money, cash, or liquidating funds. You can approach it from many angles depending on what you have available to you. In many ways, the simplest is to use the cash you have on hand and go with conventional financing. That is how we bought our first one.

With all three of our homes, we have used different tactics, but the first one was with 25% down and by funding the remodel out of pocket. For our second one, we put the cash down by taking out a HELOC on our primary home and paid for the remaining furnishings and housewares out of pocket. For our third, we used private money and will refinance into a commercial or traditional loan within the first year. There is no right or wrong answer, but each financing option has its own quirks to be aware of. So, if you don't feel like you have enough cash on hand, there are other options to get started on your short term rental!

Option 1: Traditional Financing

This is often referred to as conventional financing. This means it falls within conforming loan criteria for residential mortgage loans. In this case, you could do a conventional loan deemed as an investment or a second home. These products will vary from area to area and lender to lender, so it is something you need to talk about with your loan officer or bank.

If you go the route of a conventional investment loan, then you likely will need to put 20%-25% of the purchase price down as your downpayment. The closing timeline for these loans is generally around thirty days, sometimes less and sometimes more, depending on who is providing the loan. You can also potentially do a conventional second home loan, which can require as little as 10% down. Those loans have some quirks to them in terms of the distance of your primary home and how often you can or can't use the home.

Option 2: Commercial Loan

Since your short term rental is going to be a business, you may qualify for a commercial loan. The major benefit of these loans is that they generally are not personally guaranteed. They are lending based on the business plan and projected revenue. These loans don't show up on your credit report, which makes it easier to get future conventional loans. The drawback is that they tend to be more expensive by having higher rates and shorter terms. So, they make for a great temporary option if you intend to pay the property off quickly.

Option 3: Cash

If you happen to have available cash funds, then you can bankroll this purchase and start up with that money. Your cash can come from your savings, a stock portfolio, or other personal accounts.

Option 4: HELOC

If you have a property already, then you could take out a home equity line of credit on that property based on the equity that you have in it. These are referred to as HELOCs. Each lending institution will have its own requirements and restrictions, but they can be a great option to leverage your current property to get you started with your investment. They generally aren't used for long-term financing because their interest rates vary but they can be great for a short term option to get into a property.

In many cases, the bank lending this line of credit will have a loan limit of $200,000-$400,000. It will depend on your finances, your equity position, and the institution's lending abilities. This product can be great if you are planning to purchase a property, renovate it, and then refinance into a conventional loan, but that is a strategy discussion for another book.

With all of these options, you may be asking yourself, where do these different loans come from? Simply put, a mortgage broker is the route that we have gone for our conventional loans. Other places you can go include a national or local bank loan officer, a commercial lender, and a local bank or credit union for a HELOC.

Once you have your financing secured, you will be ready to start seriously shopping and submit an offer. If you are at this point, then you likely already have hired a real estate Agent, or you should be looking for one. Keep in mind, not all Agents are created equal. A great Agent is going to be your trusted resource and guide. As an Agent myself, I will tell you that committing to an Agent and following their lead through the process will make everything go smoothly. Work with an Agent who is familiar with the area, which means that they understand the data trends for pricing, days on the market, what can be negotiated during the offer process, and what looks like a good long term investment to meet your goals.

If you already have an Agent you like to work with and they feel like they can represent you in the market you want to buy into, stick with them. Developing trust with your Agent is the biggest key to a successful real estate transaction. If your regular Agent isn't able to help you in a specific market, then ask them to refer you to an Agent in that market. This is huge! Especially if you really like to work with them, they will be able to find an Agent that will work similarly to them and take care of you in a familiar way.

When it comes to making an offer, here is what to generally expect. Your deal will be structured based on many things:

+ Price
+ Closing timeline
+ Earnest money
+ Contingencies
+ Financing

You will determine your offer price based on what is fair or a "good deal" in that market at the time. The closing timeline is a large part of getting the deal done in terms of enticing the Seller, which is second to price but sometimes more important. Depending on the Seller's position,

Chapter 7: The Deal

they may want a quick close under 30 days, if possible, or they may need a longer close to find their next place to go. Finding out what would be most valuable to the Seller is going to be your biggest lever to agree on your most desirable price.

Another term that will be considered by the Seller is the amount of earnest money deposit you are putting down. This is different from your down payment, but it does get applied to it at closing. Your Agent should be able to guide you in how much you are willing and able to put up as a deposit to show good faith. The rule of thumb is usually 1% unless it's more competitive. Sometimes, the best leverage is to make the earnest money non-refundable after the inspection or appraisal has been satisfied. At the end of the day, you should be able to rely on your Agent to guide you through the process of writing the most solid offer based on market conditions and the property.

Your offer will likely have multiple contingencies that will protect your earnest money deposit and spell out exactly how the contract should be executed. These include but are not limited to financing, inspections, title, and feasibility. The financing contingency is a major contingency if you are securing a loan for the purchase. Each state or Multiple Listing Service (known as the MLS) will have a different version of its financing addendum but, generally, this is one of the most robust contingencies to protect your earnest money and an escape strategy to get you out of the deal in the event that you aren't able to close the loan for the home for some unforeseen reason.

The next most full-coverage contingency is the inspection phase. In many cases, the inspection contingency is your get-out-of-jail-free card. Depending on the nuances of the market you are buying in, this can be the easiest way to back out of a deal if you get cold feet or have findings during the inspection that make the property not a good deal or fit for you any longer.

Maybe more comes up than you were expecting and it is more than you can handle. You can generally terminate the contract at this point and get your earnest money deposit back. That being said, make sure to ask your Agent how the contract works and at what point you can back out of the contract if needed, if at all. Keep in mind that you should never enter into a contract unless you intend to proceed. It is a legally binding document, so you don't want to take it lightly. Make sure you also understand how you can exit the contract if needed.

Often, you also have a title contingency and, in most areas, the contract will make sure that having a clear title is part of the contract prior to closing. That is the job of the title company throughout the escrow/transaction process. However, many contracts will have an option for the Buyer to review the title information ahead of time and back out if there is anything on the title report that is not satisfactory to them. For instance, perhaps there is an easement that wasn't previously disclosed and you aren't comfortable with a neighbor crossing your property at their leisure to access the beach.

Lastly, it may make more sense to include a feasibility contingency. Since this is a purchase for an investment, a feasibility period may be a good option to encompass many of the already mentioned contingencies. This is a period of time where the Buyer can complete any and all due diligence including an inspection, making sure the market stats and numbers make sense, and looking into permitting and local requirements. This type of contingency is more of a pass or fail hurdle. In this case, you have a set amount of time, say 15 days, to get the home under contract and complete any homework you need to in order to feel comfortable moving to close. At any point, if you decide that it won't work for you, then you can give a notice of dissatisfaction. In the event that you get to the end of the study and want to proceed, then your

Chapter 7: The Deal

feasibility is satisfied and you generally can move swiftly to closing. This is more common with commercial lending and land purchases, but could also apply to a short term rental. The commonality of this contingency being used will be determined by the local nuances.

After all of your contingencies are satisfied, your next stop will be closing. The timeline will vary depending on when the Seller can be out of the property, when the financing can be finalized, and whatever is agreeable to both parties. This can take as quick as a few days for a cash sale, or as long as a couple of months to close on your property. Traditionally, if you are getting a conventional loan for the property, the sale closes in 30-45 days to leave enough time for due diligence and for the loan to get finalized. What it all boils down to is all contingencies being satisfied, the title being cleared, and funds being received in order to be able to disperse them on closing day. When it comes to closing, you will either sign papers ahead of time and wire the funds for your downpayment and closing costs to escrow, or an attorney firm prior to closing depending on how your state handles things. Then, the day of closing is all a formality for those funds to be released and for the sale to be recorded with the local municipality.

In the case of our purchases, we have bought one property without furniture and two with furniture. It is good to note that this was part of our negotiations with the purchase price, but when it comes to having the property appraised, it does not include the value of the furniture. For the two homes we bought furnished, there wasn't an exact percentage or value placed on the furnishings, but my valuation was that it saved us about $10,000 and about a week in labor time.

In our contracts, our lender suggested that we note that all personal property is being conveyed at no value just to avoid any issues with lending. You may also have the opportunity to buy the furnishings outside of the purchase and sale agreement. Again, this is something that your Agent will be able to help you with. In our case, it was great to buy the homes furnished so that we could remove anything we didn't want in there, add things we needed, replace linens, and simplify decor. In our second property, we also ended up changing out a lot of light fixtures, which really changed the feel of the space from builder basic to luxury cabin.

My hope for sharing about the transaction process is that you will have a better idea of how the process goes and the types of things that you should be considering when you are purchasing a short term rental. Whether you have bought and sold properties often or never, it is always wise to get a detailed understanding of the process from a real estate professional. I do not recommend going it alone because you will likely end up leaving money on the table or experiencing a very bumpy road to closing. No one wants to start their exciting new investment journey out on the wrong foot, so hire a professional and enjoy the process of becoming an investor.

Part 2:
Let's Get Geared Up

Chapter 8:
Cast Your Vision

Now let the fun begin! This is where you get to let the creative juices flow in terms of what you want your rental to be, as I am sure you have already been scheming. In this chapter, you will be dreaming about what your ideal guest will be like, what they will be interested in, and what activities they will be partaking in during their stay. This will influence your design choices, amenities, and layout of the property.

So, let's start with WHO you will be hosting most often.

Your ideal guest is who you want to refer back to any time you come to a crossroads in your design plan or when it comes to choosing amenities to provide. You cannot please everyone, so the more that your rental is niched down to a certain type of traveler then the more successful it will be.

For instance, when it comes to our ocean rentals, we chose properties that provide enough space for a large family, a couple of small families, or groups because there was a need in that market. Knowing that we would be catering to groups led us to the types of amenities that we would need to provide. In my opinion, a fully functional kitchen with all the cook and bakeware was crucial, because I wanted people to be able to celebrate holidays there. We also needed to keep in mind that our houses are by the beach, which means sand—lots of sand! So, when we were remodeling, we kept in mind what materials would do best under the conditions of having families, kids, and dogs in our home after a trip to the beach. Next up, we wanted to have comfortable sleeping conditions for groups or families. We made soft, comfortable bedding a priority and included at least one pack n' play for those bringing the littlest of travelers along with them.

Let's address WHAT the space should be.

Once you have nailed down who is going to be staying, envision what the space should look like. Here are some questions to get you thinking:

+ What would they love and appreciate about their ideal rental?
+ Is there a theme in the area that will influence your decor and style of the interior?
+ Are there certain colors that make the most sense and are complimentary of the area?
+ How many people will the home sleep, or should it sleep?
+ Will this be a place for groups, solo travelers, or pairs?
+ How long will their stay generally be?
+ What amenities should you provide that would make their stay extra special or comfortable?

All of these things will attract the type of guest that you are aiming to host, down to the amount of nightly rent that they are able and willing to pay.

In our case of being on the coast where many people fish, crab, and clam, we made sure to have a fish cleaning table set up so they have a designated area for that task. It also keeps them from cleaning fish guts in our beautiful kitchen!

When it comes to the design of the space, you want to make sure it matches the location and destination vibe in some way while also being functional. I have viewed and stayed in places that were too over-the-top with a theme to the point where nothing was actually comfortable or quality. I am all about socials and an epic backdrop, but going overboard will actually deter more guests than it will gain them. Swinging chairs are cool but also think about their durability and the likelihood of them causing damage to the house—or worse, to a guest.

Let's discuss HOW to make this possible.

Along these same lines, if you are going to be hosting people in a spot that is known for hiking, you will want to leave coffee table books that provide trail information and suggestions. Adding a space for hiking gear to be hung, dropped, or stored is also a nice touch to allow people to dry their gear and keep your house a bit cleaner during their stay. If your home is in wine country, team up with a local car service that will pick guests up and drop them off after a day of tasting. You don't even have to provide a discount code—although that would be ideal—but having a reliable contact and having that company know you and your property will make the experience that much better. I have found that just having good resources for guests is the real win over providing a discounted rate.

My philosophy on design is that less is more when it comes to vacation rentals. You don't want things cluttering your space, but you do want it to feel comfortable and homey. You also want to make it easy for your cleaners to keep it in a good, clean condition between stays. Dream up a space that is clean, comfortable, and on theme with the area and you will have never-ending bookings!

At this point, you probably have already been dreaming about your short term rental location, what it will look like and feel like, and the types of activities that your guests will enjoy. You are most likely catering to guests who are just like you! When my husband and I were outfitting our first rental, we had different priorities for what we should provide to make the guest experience better. For instance, my husband is an avid outdoorsman so he was thinking about all the things we could provide for crabbing, fishing, and clam-digging. I knew that was what was bringing people to our home, but I had other amenities in mind.

So, it was his idea to make a space for those guests to clean their seafood at our house without it being in our beautiful new kitchen. We made a space with a stainless steel table, tubs, water, and buckets near the garbage for our guests to be able to process their fresh catch. Genius! It was much appreciated by both our guests and our housekeepers.

Meanwhile, I was thinking about how to make it comfortable for groups of people ranging from grandparents to babies. Both of our approaches and priorities were valid and important because we were thinking about how we would want to enjoy this sleepy beach town with our families. From fishing to relaxing, we wanted everyone to be set up for a great stay.

For a quick activity, I want you to write down an ideal day at your desired vacation market. What is the itinerary of events? When will you wake up? What will breakfast, lunch, and day activities look like? What will dinner be like? How does the day end? Once you have your perfect day mapped out, write down amenities and must-haves that would make that day possible, most enjoyable, and epic. I will talk about guest guides later in the book, but this itinerary you just wrote down should be included and your property should reflect that vibe throughout this whole journey. Bottle up that essence and refer back to it at every turn in this process.

Chapter 9:
Own Your Role

This chapter is all about you and your part to play in making your investment a success both financially and personally. Your short term rental should make you money, allow you to take advantage of tax benefits, and give you a place to enjoy with friends and family. That being said, it will add more to your plate of responsibility but within reason. You will soon find out that I am a big proponent of self-management, but I know that this is not reasonable or a great option for many. However, I do believe it is attainable for more people than one may think. Just like the thought of buying and owning a short term rental can seem far-fetched or a dream that won't ever actually be a reality, I think that self-management is the same way. More on that later!

The number one thing that has made me most effective in business and as a mom is committing to owning my role, my strengths, and the things I personally need to do while outsourcing the rest. Now that we have gone over what you are going to be buying and you have built out the plan for your space, you need to cast your vision for what you are actually going to be responsible for going forward. Many first-time investors are afraid to spend too much money, which is great to not get yourself in a bad position, but you will make a lot more money if you stay in your strength zone as much as possible. Then you resolve to hire people who are better than you to handle the things that you aren't great at or can't easily accomplish for whatever reason whether it is your skill, location, etc. I will go back to the example of being realistic about the type of DIY projects you can take on since the same applies here. You will do more damage to your overall goals if you get too off into the weeds in areas that you just aren't competent in.

Okay, so what am I really talking about? Many responsibilities will need attention when you are in the process of getting your home launched and dealing with the ongoing management. I will dive into each of these roles in more detail in the next chapter, but to overview some of your future needs, you will need a designer, stylist, various contractors (painter, plumber, electrician, woodworker, etc.), house manager, handyman, cleaner, groundskeeper, and specialty vendors (for hot tubs, windows, and general maintenance).

You know that your space will need a design, be furnished, get some painting and cleaning, maybe get some new flooring, and so on. So, how much of that will you be handling yourself? Who else will be involved? Will you have a partner? Are you doing this with your spouse? Maybe you have a skilled friend that you are going to bring in during the launch phase to help with design and styling.

After answering those questions, determine what you are capable of executing, what your team would be great at, and who else you will need on your team to get to the finish line. Keep in mind, you can be the project manager or you can be the contractor, so this is your opportunity to save yourself money in the future by preventing early maintenance or repairs. Doing it right from the beginning will save you a lot of headaches down the road!

As you read that list and answered those questions, what things did you immediately grasp onto as a task that you would or could handle?

Chapter 9: Own Your Role

When did you say, "Hmm, I will need someone for that"? Without thinking about it too much, you already have an intuition about what is reasonable for you to handle and what you need to outsource.

When it comes to our short term rentals, my husband and I divide many of these tasks between the two of us and then we hire the rest as needed. When we were renovating our first rental, we hired my uncle to help with the construction. Also, my father-in-law helped with painting and other tasks, our friends joined in with some renovation projects and design, and my sister and Mom chipped in with painting and the final installation of furniture. It can take a village. Your need for additional help or hires will greatly depend on what type of project you are embarking on. Sometimes the people you need on your team are there for your kids. If you have kids and you are trying to get your rental up and running, you will need childcare for multiple days or weekends. Who are those people going to be?

For many of the ongoing maintenance and repair items that come up, my husband can absolutely handle them, but he also works a 9-5, so driving the two hours each way to wash windows doesn't really make sense. So, we have a window person that washes the windows a couple of times a year. We also find that when we go down to work on the properties, we have many other tasks that he prefers to handle himself that take precedence over cleaning out the gutters. So, again, we hire that out and handle the other specialty situations and repairs. Although my husband handles many of the repair items, we still have a handyman in both locations that we can call on in the event something comes up between our maintenance visits. And unexpected or immediate repair needs do come up.

Keep in mind, this is just what works for us. The roles and responsibilities that you are hoping and able to take on may vary from ours, and that is great! This should be tailored to what works for you and your business. There will also be things that you might not be stellar at, but they fall into your responsibility category either because you haven't found a person to hire or you don't have it in your budget to outsource, so it makes more sense for you to handle it for now. This type of investing takes critical thinking skills and the ability to pivot. Sometimes, you just have to get things done and take matters into your own hands even if it isn't ideal.

I can't stress this enough: When it comes to doing something yourself, please, please, please do not allow it to look like you did it yourself. You do not want people saying, "Well, it definitely looks like they did this themselves..." Make sure that your finished product is well done. Don't bite off more than you can chew and be realistic with yourself. The savings of DIY get costly when things aren't done well and you eventually have to hire a professional to do it right the next time.

Everyone's threshold is going to be different in terms of what time they can spend on their rental business and what they can commit to for the management role. I can guarantee that when you buy your first one, you will spend a lot more time fussing over it than is actually necessary. If you end up buying more, you will realize that you didn't need to spend as much time looking at the competition as you did. Once you do your initial market research, you really only need to check in with what the other competition is doing about once a quarter. You will want to visit your nightly pricing if things aren't getting booked consistently, but you don't need to obsess over it. What I am really trying to say is that you will be like an excited puppy with your first STR and obsess over all the things—number of bookings, revenue, competition, tiny furnishing details, etc. Then, once you add more to your portfolio, you will gain a different perspective that allows you to stay in a big picture mindset more often.

Please don't read that last sentence and think that I said that you don't need to think about the details of your vacation home because you absolutely do. The details are what make your guest's experience next level and a customer for life. But we do tend to get carried away with unimportant details far too often when we are new investors and anxiously waiting for our investment to turn a profit.

As I take you on this journey to reveal your role in your rental business, you will undoubtedly need to bring people into your business to fill the gaps. Imagine that you are in escrow on your vacation rental. Take a moment to write down the things that you will be handling, who you want to bring into the project, and what contractors you need to look into hiring. The few weeks that you are in escrow serve as the perfect planning time so that as soon as you close you can hit the ground running.

Keep in mind I said "planning," not "buying." If you are getting financing for the property, do not go out and start spending on materials and furniture until AFTER you have closed on the property. You don't want your debt-to-income ratio to be affected and make things harder or impossible to get through the underwriting process. But you should be seeking out where you can get the best-priced materials and interviewing contractors. That way, you won't be mentally bogged down with those details when it is go-time.

When you decide that you are up for the job of self-management, you need to be clear on the amount of effort and time that you can put into communications with your guests. You also need to be there for your vendors when ordering supplies and approving repairs. When it comes to knowing when supplies are needed or what repairs are necessary, I rely on my house managers. They are there getting "boots on the ground" intel about what the house needs, how guests left your property, and if there is anything that needs attention before the next guest or in the near future. This person is the only way that you will be able to manage from afar, so you want to make sure that you are a great communicator, fair and respectful of their time and efforts, and can keep both a happy relationship and a beautiful property.

As you go through the process of launching your rental and getting into the management of the property, you will want to periodically check in with yourself about the roles that you are fulfilling, including what is working, what isn't, and if there are any areas where you should be shifting responsibility. Maybe you hired a house manager but they actually aren't doing much, so you can take on those tasks and just lean on the cleaner to know when you are short on supplies. Or maybe you have been manually writing the check-in instructions for each guest and it is time to set up an auto-response for the day of arrival. Again, you will need the ability to critically assess what is working and what is not as an ongoing practice so that you know when to pivot and make this investment a success. Most importantly, own your role! This is where the magic will happen.

Chapter 10:
To Self-Manage or Not To Self-Manage, That Is The Question

When it comes to the management of your property, you have two choices. You can choose to self-manage with the help of a house manager, or you can hire a property management company. A property management company will already be ready with its own plan to launch your listing, handle reservations, and coordinate cleaning and repairs. Self-managing, on the other hand, will take a bit of a learning curve.

If you are thinking that you want to hire a property management company, it is likely because you are afraid of the time dedication that you need to commit to in order to manage it yourself. You don't want to recreate the wheel and you want a professional company who has done this hundreds of times to deal with all of the continuing business needs. You are seeking a passive source of income.

I, too, had those feelings when we expanded to a new market that was twice as far away from home, so I caved to the perceived notion that I couldn't manage it from that far away, even though I started with self-management and had a great experience.

If a property management company is what you want to explore, then here are some things I learned from the two companies that I worked with in the past. First, their contract terms will vary. Some will be annual, some will be multi-year, and some you will be able to cancel at any time where they have a 90-day period to slowly pull their management and reservations. Still others you can cancel immediately for a fee.

Second, their fees will range from 12-40% of the booking revenue. They will also charge the guest the cleaning fee as part of the reservation. Most often, they have a program where they charge you as the homeowner for the restocking supplies so you don't have to order things like soap, toilet paper, paper towels, shampoo, conditioner, etc. This is usually charged per stay and billed monthly.

Lastly, they will have an online portal so you can look at the calendar, block dates that you plan on using the home, and track reservations and revenue. If this set-it-and-forget-it route is for you, then I would also recommend shopping around, asking for references of current owners, and having an attorney review the contract before entering into a business relationship with them. You will want to know your way out of the contract if you get a couple or a few months into it and realize that it isn't a good fit for you, your property, and your business plan.

Also, talk to your tax professional about the pros and cons of hiring a management company. By hiring a property management company for your STR, you won't be eligible for certain tax benefits. That may not matter to you, or it may cause you to think again about self-management.

If you are thinking that you want to go the route of hiring a property management company because you don't have the time to be that active in this investment or don't have the bandwidth to build out systems with a house manager, then that is perfectly fine. You should explore hiring a company. If that is the direction you want to go, then you will need to be comfortable with not having as much control over your home, how things are done, and what type of products they stock.

Chapter 10: To Self-Manage or Not To Self-Manage, That Is The Question

Management companies run their rentals a certain way with their specific systems and it will not be tailored to what you want your guests' experience to be or to your home's needs. This absolutely makes sense since they are running a business with tens, hundreds, or thousands of properties and it is humanly impossible for them to tailor each property in a customized way. They have to maintain rigid systems in order to scale. Let me be clear—it is wonderful if that works for you. It just didn't work for me. I have a certain experience that I want my guests to have and standards of care that I want as a renter.

When you are embarking on the journey of being a short term rental owner, you will need to consider what direction will work best for you. At this point, you have likely gleaned that, in my ideal world, you will self-manage by hiring a house manager. In my view, it is the best of both worlds. You can set up systems to your liking and delegate tasks that specifically work for you, your time allotment, your skill sets, and your proximity to the property. Of course, that means that you are managing a person, but if you hire right then it will be far better than any experience with a large company.

If hiring a company sounds too restrictive or not what you envisioned during your business planning phase, then maybe self-managing will be a better fit. As it stands, I self-manage all three of our vacation rentals. Our homes are two hours and four hours away from our home, so I have hired house managers in both locations. I will talk more about my management style in the coming chapters, but ultimately I control everything that can be done remotely—the listings, reservation management, guest care, supply purchasing, and any work that needs to be done.

So, now that you know my political view (that was a joke), I will also say that just because that is how I like to run my short term rental investments, I also totally understand if it is not desirable or viable for many people. I also want to be clear that it does not mean you aren't a good fit for short term rentals! Many people are perfectly happy with hiring a management company and I hope that there are better options for you in your market than there are for me in mine. I just want to make it known that, with the right hires, self-management is more attainable than you may think.

It is hard for me to quantify the hours that I spend managing because the work fits well into my daily routine and workflow. If I were to venture a guess, I would say that I spend about 8 hours a week talking with guests, working with the house managers, reviewing pricing, updating listings, and ordering supplies. Some weeks, if an issue arises, then there will be more communication necessary. During other weeks, we will spend a couple of days at the rentals getting them spruced up or spending time doing repairs. Still other weeks, I have limited work to do during the low seasons. The workflow is familiar to me given my day job as a real estate Agent, so it doesn't add a huge amount of obligation to my already unpredictable schedule.

If you are now intrigued by how I actually self-manage, then hang on for the future section. You are heading into the part of the book that will cover how I manage my short term rentals in detail. Even if this is something that you plan to outsource to a company, I am sure that you will find it insightful to know what is going on behind the scenes for whomever you have hired to run your property. Let's dive in and meet your team.

Chapter 11:
Meet The Team

I briefly touched on the type of roles and vendors involved in a short term rental previously. In this chapter, I will deep dive into who is needed, when they are needed, and how to execute their role. To circle back on the list of potential hires, you will need to include a designer, stylist, painter, plumber, electrician, woodworker, house manager, handyman, cleaner, groundskeeper, and specialty vendors for things like the hot tub, windows, and general maintenance.

The secret is to hire people into these roles who can potentially act in multiple capacities. If your cleaner can double as the person checking on your supplies or is able to drop off supplies for guests if something comes up during their stay, then that is a huge win. If you buy a short term rental out of the area, then you will need some fantastic people that act as your boots on the ground.

Before you get into hiring people for those management positions, you will likely need to hire contractors during your build-out phase. I also want to make it clear that I mention hiring a variety of different roles, but it doesn't mean that you have to or will need to hire each one of those types of vendors. It all depends on your property and its needs. If your role is going to be styling and decor, then great! You don't need to hire someone to do that, but it is still a role that needs to be filled in one way or another.

In my case, I had a friend with a background in staging and styling help me with the final touches of our first short term rental. This was super helpful after I had gone through stocking the essentials, ordered all of the necessary furnishings, and put them together. I needed a second set of eyes to really pull everything together and make sure it was photo and guest ready.

Keep in mind that many of these hires will be working simultaneously. You can be working on your roles of designing and ordering furniture while your handyman is on the property checking off tasks and the painter gives the whole place a fresh new color vibe.

There are a number of tasks that we have handled ourselves but that you may want to hire. For example, you may need to switch out the light fixtures because they can make a huge impact on your space and design. It is also a good idea to switch out old toilets, or at least replace the wax seal to ensure that you won't have a leaky toilet in the near future that would jeopardize new flooring. Maybe you envision a built-in bunk bed, so you need to hire a woodworker for the construction. Then, of course, there is general contracting work like siding repair, window repair, tub caulking, and any other things that need to be buttoned up before it is ready to rent.

For us, many of these tasks were taken on by my husband, who doubles as my business partner. In most cases, they would be hired out. For the things that you are able to do yourself, just make sure that the finished product is well done. Do not bite off more than you can chew. If you don't have it done correctly from the start, then you risk having it cause more issues for you down the road. At that point, you will likely have to hire a professional to come and fix it later, which is more time, money, and potentially a temporary delay in keeping you from renting your home out.

After you have hired the vendors to get your property ready, you will now need to make your most important team hire—your house manager. This person can do a wide variety of tasks and their role can be built out to best suit you, your needs, and your property needs. It is very important to get clear on what their role will be.

Things to consider:

+ Will they be managing the property listings?
+ Will they coordinate other vendors such as house cleaners, window washers, landscapers, and handymen?
+ How close do they live to the property and how familiar are they with the area?
+ What will they get paid for the role?
+ How will they be paid? Hourly? Every turn? Monthly?
+ Are there other homes they are managing? How many?
+ Do they have the proper time and bandwidth to tend to your property?

All of these things can be fluid to match your needs and may vary from property to property.

For instance, we have handled house management in different ways during our experience. For two of the properties, the owner of the cleaning company acts as our house manager and keeps track of maintenance, repair needs, and supply replenishment. I have often sent her supplies to restock the homes if I am unable to deliver them myself. This service is included in the cleaning fee that we get charged and we get billed every two weeks for any cleaning, repairs, or maintenance.

Your manager is your catalyst for how well your property gets booked and absolutely for how well it gets reviewed. The way that I show them respect is by being responsive when they have a need. If they don't have supplies, they can't do their job, which is very frustrating. If your washer and dryer are old and small, it makes getting the laundry turned over exponentially harder and, of course, takes more time. If they are wasting time waiting around to get it done, then it makes it more difficult for them to get to other properties or to hit the check-in times.

For a specific example, we bought a new large washer and dryer set for our first rental because right after we started renting it out, it was clear they were not going to cut it for the cleaning crew and the amount of laundry that it takes between guests of a home that sleeps ten people. When it comes to being fair, sometimes you need to give your staff the benefit of the doubt if a guest reports something displeasing to them that they could have avoided. Your cleaners are real people with their own lives and stresses and every cleaning is not going to be perfect. Give them a little grace, but also keep track of negative patterns. Lastly, communicate with them often. Make sure that you fully understand any issues that are arising and who else they may be hiring to service your property. If you get the same concerning feedback then you will know you have an issue to resolve.

You are working with your cleaning crew and house manager as a team, together. The way that my self-management works is that I handle the listings, bookings, guest communications, licensing, supply buying, and other odds and ends. My crew is solely in charge of property cleaning, reporting on how guests left our home, informing me about the supplies that we need to replenish, and being on call in case they need to go to the home to resolve an issue during a guest's stay, meet a vendor, or coordinate an appointment time that works for them.

That being the case, we rely on each other to clearly state our needs and expectations just like with any other partnership. Your manager is an extension of you and is there to help make sure your guests are well taken care of during your stay. I always tell guests at check-in to report back if something isn't as they expected upon arrival because this is when my cleaning crew has the opportunity to rectify something before it ends up on a review page. It also puts them at ease when I quickly get an issue handled. This is another reason why I highly recommend self-management with a house manager because they can react quickly but larger companies can be hard to get a hold of or hard to get someone out to the house when an in-person solution is necessary.

In another instance, we have a house manager who is separate from the cleaner and manages both the cleaning schedule and quality control. She gets paid a separate fee from the hourly cleaning charge.

Regardless of the direction in which you go, it needs to match up with your expectations and time availability. My preference is to be very hands-on by taking care of our listings, communicating with guests, and staying in the loop with my house manager to ensure that everything is as it should be. However, many people prefer to be more hands-off, and that is great, too. Whatever works for you and your investment goals is the way to go.

The other regular hires that you will need on your team include your cleaner—if they aren't part of your house management hire, a handyman, and a groundskeeper. The other vendors that you may need include pest control, hot tub and pool technician, window washer, and professional photographer. These hires are not necessarily your regularly scheduled folks, but they are contacts that you need in your back pocket. If you have a hot tub or pool, you will want those vendors scheduled for regular maintenance. We have our hot tub person come tend to the hot tub every two weeks and as needed.

Here are some other things that you will want to consider when you hire your cleaner:

+ Have they done or do they already do short term rentals?
+ Are they used to handling bedding, linens, and restocking supplies?
+ Are they going to be able to report when you need more supplies or if things are missing, broken, or in need of repairs?

Make sure to communicate how you want the house left after they have turned it over. I have sent my cleaners the link to the property listing so they can see from the photos exactly how I want things set up. It is amazing how guests move decor and furniture around, and it drives me nuts when I come for a property visit and things aren't as I expect them to be. So, it is very helpful to have a cleaning staff who can help keep things in order. You will also need them to report back to you after each clean so that you can fill out the guest review on the various portals such as Airbnb.

Next up, your handyman. You need someone local so they can be on standby for guest emergency repairs. Things happen and it pays off in raving reviews if you can get someone over there to address any issues in a timely manner. No one wants to be inconvenienced on vacation and it is our duty as a Host to avoid that at all costs, within reason. Your handyman will also be crucial for ongoing maintenance and in making sure your property stays in good condition. With lots of guest turnover, you want to keep up with repairs and maintenance so things don't get destroyed.

Lastly, as I like to call them, the groundskeeper. You may not need a full-blown landscaper for every property. It could be the neighbor who mows the lawn regularly, but you need someone to maintain the grounds to make sure the property is in a presentable and enjoyable condition for your guests. I am talking lawn service, weed control, and bi-annual yard clean-up. When it comes to short term rentals, presentation matters!

Depending on your location in the world, you may need other regular specialty vendors than the ones I mentioned, but, for the most part, these are your major players. If you have a seasoned, local house manager, they will likely be able to connect you with other people who they have worked with in the past. They may even keep some of their own staff. Building out your team will ensure that your property is a wild success.

Chapter 12:
Outfitting The Space

Now, let's get down to how to actually set up your rental. In this chapter, I will cover all of the nitty-gritty details about things that you need, or at least need to consider having in your rental. I will go over the things that we added to ours to make our guest experience better and what we left out in order to avoid future issues. This will go beyond the fun design aspects. This will cover safety, compliance, and necessities along with where I source things from and how to continually restock our homes. This will be the chapter that you refer back to time and time again as you get your properties outfitted. I will also have a checklist at the end so that you can go ahead and get my curated list for purchases and keep an inventory list. My opinion is that a well-stocked kitchen and quality bedding will give you happy guests time and time again. You want this to be their home away from home—or maybe even better!

When it comes to your inventory list, you will be able to use many of the things on my list, but, of course, you will need to tailor it to your own property needs. It is a very good idea to take note of everything that you put in the house to start with and then update the list at least once a quarter to keep on top of replacements and missing items. This is something that you or your house manager can do. You would be surprised what things walk away after the peak season comes and goes.

For some reason, all of our acrylic glassware disappeared— Not to worry, I will cover this more in a later chapter and explain how to handle these types of situations with guests.

The big basic items that every property will need are kitchenware and linens. When it comes to linens, my rule of thumb is to have three sheet sets per bed, including duvet covers. This is so that you can have one clean set in use, one getting washed, and a spare just in case. I tend to use quilts on top of down-alternative duvets with white duvet covers. In my experience, this simple design keeps things looking fresh and the materials are easy to clean and remove as necessary.

You need to have mattress covers. I buy the ones off of Amazon that are waterproof but don't sound like you are sleeping on plastic. This is to keep your mattresses as hygienic as possible, cut down on allergens, and keep away bed bugs. The same goes for pillows—every pillow needs a pillow cover in addition to cases.

Next up, towels. You can never have enough towels. I order bulk sets in white because these are the most highly replaced items in our properties. In an ideal world, I would love to provide super soft, plush towels, but the truth of the matter is that they go missing or get ruined, so we have to keep re-ordering them. To this day, no one has commented about the quality of our towels. Note: I buy white because they are easy to bleach.

We don't provide beach towels at the request of our housekeeping staff because laundering linens is the thing that takes the longest during a cleaning turn. So, we ask guests to bring their own beach towels and towels for their pets. I have three towel sets per person that the home sleeps, so you can make one to two towels of each variety available for each guest. If your home sleeps ten like mine, you need at least thirty towels of each size—face, hand, and body. While we are on the topic of towels and linens, don't forget that you also need kitchen towels and cleaning cloths. Both are easily ordered in bulk.

When it comes to outfitting your kitchen, my opinion is that you need everything that you need to make a holiday meal. It doesn't really matter what type of holiday meal, but, in my head, I always imagine having everything necessary to cook Thanksgiving dinner and everything else that comes along with that.

Start your list (or check out mine) with the basics: You will need at least one dinner plate, salad plate, bowl, coffee cup, water glass, cocktail glass, and an assortment of wine glasses for the number of guests that your home sleeps, but ideally two of each. Since people are vacationing, I also like to provide acrylic plates and cups for eating outside. This will hopefully also cut down on the number of glasses and plates that get broken. I also like to get silverware sets in bulk so I can provide at least double the occupancy rate for utensils.

Now it is time to think about what guests will need to cook, prepare, and present a nice meal to a group of people. This is where you want to think about a crockpot, baking sheets, mixing bowls, a hand or stand mixer, muffin tins, bread molds, pie plate, large salad bowl, an assortment of platters and serving bowls, glass baking ware, roasting pan, spatulas, wood cooking utensils, grill utensils, and, of course, a full set of pots and pans. I usually go for one of the sets at Costco. If you go with non-stick in anything, it will need to be replaced every couple of years, but they hold up pretty well if people don't scratch them.

Then there are your appliance essentials: blender, coffee pot—Keurig, Nespresso, pour over, French press, or whatever you are into, tea kettle, maybe a coffee grinder, a good set of regular knives, and a set of steak knives. Other helpful things we have included are strainers, toasters, food storage containers, hot pads and hot mitts, and lots of cutting boards! Making sure that you have everything a guest could ever need will make a huge difference. Our top two compliments from guests are, number one, how well-stocked our kitchens are and, number two, how comfortable our beds and bedding are.

Once you have all the things your guests will need to cook comfortably, you will want to add some cooking supplies to make their stay even better. We provide coffee, tea, sugar, honey, olive oil, REAL salt and pepper in grinders (not the crappy finely ground stuff), foil, plastic wrap, Ziplock bags, paper plates, disposable cups, and lighters. We often also have steak seasoning there. Many people bring their own supplies, and I do suggest that they do if they are picky about the coffee type or tea brand, but it does make it a lot easier for guests to be able to settle into their stay and get cooking, especially if they forgot something. It is lovely to have it in the home and save them a trip to the store. My opinion is to forego the guest gift and splurge on a one-time purchase that your guests will actually enjoy and use!

Now onto the other areas of the home that need to be outfitted. It can be a daunting task to outfit a whole home, so the way that I have broken it down is room by room. I also remind myself that less is more. You want your space to be comfortable and clean, not cluttered. This will make it appear better in your photos for your listing, will be easier for your cleaners to keep sparkling clean, and will allow guests to feel at ease with a simple yet cozy space for their stay.

For all of the things that I mentioned above, I mainly bought them from Amazon and Bed, Bath, and Beyond. It makes it quite simple to have your list of things to buy and then just type into the search bar on Amazon and have your pick of brands and pricing. The same goes for Bed, Bath, & Beyond. When I was outfitting the first property, it made it

Chapter 12: Outfitting The Space

easy to jog my memory on what we needed by walking through a store that was laid out room by room.

Lucky for you, you have my list of suggested items, but, if you are a visual person or want to add in some things that you personally love, a store like Bed, Bath, & Beyond is a great place to grab gadgets and be able to physically touch the product before you source it for your home. On the checklist, you will find out that I buy our linens and less-used furniture items from Amazon. I would classify less-used furniture as side tables and nightstands. I also buy things like boot trays, entry mats, and small rugs. Overall, there are odds and ends that I could buy at a store like Target but will probably find for a better or bulk price on Amazon.

My favorite place to source from is called At Home. We have one about 45 minutes from our house and it is a large warehouse of everything HOME. This is for sure where I like to buy art and wall décor because their selection and variety are second to none. I also have bought bar stools, pillows, kitchenware, lamps, and some décor. It is my last place during my outfitting journey to make sure that the home has everything it needs and everything to make it pop! HomeGoods is, of course, another great option for these things, but it is less predictable for what they may have and depends on what is on your to-get list. I have absolutely scored a great couch and chairs from there, and it's another great stop for pillows, décor, and kitchen needs.

For other big furniture items, I have had great luck with family members, OfferUp, Marketplace, and Craigslist. One of our most loved couches is actually a 20-year-old leather couch from my in-laws that they were getting rid of. It was super high quality, so it works perfectly in our beach house! The weathered look goes great with our home's décor and is also very sturdy and comfortable.

As you can see, we have chosen to outfit our properties with midrange furnishings for a good reason. First of all, the markets that we have our rentals in aren't high-end. Having luxury furnishings is definitely not an expectation and having high end furniture really wouldn't fit with our ideal guest. These locations attract adventurers, families, and group gatherings. Our homes are outfitted to be comfortable and clean, plus a place that you would want to return to year after year. By sourcing midrange furnishings, we stick with catering to our ideal guest and avoid breaking the bank.

All of our homes sleep ten people and cost around $15,000 to outfit. I am talking about beds, linens, kitchen stuff, dining tables, chairs, couches, lamps, decor, art, blankets, etc. Just because we aren't buying high-end or always-new furniture, that doesn't mean that they aren't quality. It is very important to us to source things that are going to withstand renters for years to come and, if we do end up with something that isn't of great quality, we find out in short order and it gets replaced.

One of our best finds for outfitting our homes is a local mattress dealer. They have all the boxed mattresses that have been returned from their free trials and are resold for a super-discounted rate. Guess what? Your guests are going to be sleeping on used mattresses anyway! They are professionally cleaned before we purchase them. This allowed us to buy six beds for half the cost of getting them new and guests ask us all the time what mattresses they are sleeping on because they are so comfortable! Finding connections like this will certainly help you keep costs down during this phase of the investment. I am sure that this exists throughout the country.

To close out the discussion of furnishings and décor, I would like to reiterate that less is more! Choose your moments to have pops of bold and an Instagramable backdrop, but always come back to what your ideal guest would enjoy so that you can bring them back for visits time and time again.

Now let's move on to the boring but crucial topic of being in compliance. Your local governing body could be your city or your county. Maybe your state has rules, too. In our case, we have a city controlling one of our markets and a county controlling the other. The two take very different approaches to their regulations.

First and foremost, find out what the rules are for having a short term rental. Do you need a permit? In order to get that permit, what will need to be done? In some of our cases, we need to have the following:

+ Annual water testing
+ Renew our permit annually
+ Site visit in order to get approved
+ Name a local representative if we don't reside close enough to the property
+ septic pumping
+ Interior postings about guest rules: quiet hours, parking, evacuation routes, emergency contacts
+ Fire extinguishers
+ Smoke and carbon monoxide detectors

Every municipality is going to have its own take on safety and their rules and regulations will likely change from year to year. You want to keep your guests as safe as possible during their stay.

My last must-have feature on all short term rentals is some type of security system and locking system that can be controlled from afar. We have exterior cameras on all of our properties and digital locks. This is something that you will want to set up and be ready to use before your home is rented. I will touch more on these details later on in the book, but you don't want to miss getting them installed at this point!

Okay, so you have made your checklist, bought all the stuff, and have everything lined up for your permit. It is now time to actually put your property together! Making it to this point, especially if you did a renovation, is SO REWARDING. It feels like you finally made it and that this investment is actually going to be a reality. Yahoo!

So, here are my pro tips on how to survive installation. First and foremost, expectations. It involves a lot of unboxing items, building furniture, cleaning kitchen items, washing sheets and towels, making beds, organizing cupboards, outfitting your cleaning closet with supply replenishment, cleaning, and placing furniture. So, needless to say, it is sweaty and you should probably count on it taking at least three days if you have great help in accomplishing all of these tasks. It is definitely a moment where you feel so excited because the moment is finally here, but it is also the sprint to the end. You want the finished product to show just how hard you have worked and just how far you have come!

It's kind of like the burst of energy you get before you are about to have a baby. Your rental is going to be birthed momentarily. Congratulations!! This also means that you don't want to skip any steps. Make sure to wash the towels and laundry that you will be storing so they are ready to go. Also, make sure to steam all of the linens so things look polished and fresh for photos and your soon-to-be guests!

So, if you are exhausted after reading this chapter, I get it. It is a lot. Sticking with the birthing analogy, it is kind of like how you forget how labor and contractions actually were and that is how your body tricks you into having more kids. I for sure forgot how much work the installation phase was until I did it a second time, and then a third time. It takes a lot of energy. But, having the finished product ready for the next phase is so

Chapter 12: Outfitting The Space

satisfying. It is a dream becoming a reality, which feels amazing! You also will only have to do this part of the phase once, so after it is outfitted and set up, you will just need to maintain and tweak it as part of your ongoing management tasks.

Are you ready to launch this thing or what?!

Use the QR code to get my inventory list!

Chapter 13:
This Is How We Do It

Self-management is a great way to make sure that your property is being managed at the level of your expectations, even if you aren't the person cleaning your property or visiting it more than once a quarter. The way this gets done is by hiring a house manager or cleaning team that will make sure the turnover between guest stays is flawless. This is where the success of your investment lies. This, of course, could be handled in a few different ways, but, in this chapter, I will share how I have had success and what things I have implemented over time to make it even better.

The best way I keep everything in smooth, working order is through our security systems. These have come in handy many times and for many reasons, especially since I am not there in real time that often. Keep in mind that since they are rentals, you have to make sure that the cameras are exterior only. We also opted for ones without audio to make guests feel more comfortable. You will need to disclose that they are on-site and whether they have audio or not as part of the listing. I have only had one guest who decided not to book just because we have cameras outside, but, in this day and age, everyone has some sort of video surveillance on their properties so it is generally a non-issue. I also think about it as a safety feature for them and for the property. Plus, you are able to monitor the check-in and check-out times of guests and the comings and goings of your cleaners or other vendors.

With that topic in mind, we did have a situation where our house manager thought we had a squatter who was messing up the house in between guest stays. That was WILD. Okay, I get how scary that sounds and it was certainly a frustrating issue that resulted in me picking up a $300 bar tab for our guests— More on how to handle unhappy guests in the next chapter. Basically what happened was a miscommunication between our manager and the cleaning team so, when the guests showed up to a VERY messy house the day before Thanksgiving, they were extremely unhappy and disgusted, to say the least. Talk about a cringy moment. There was a lot of confusion because the manager had sworn it had been cleaned but, at this moment, those details were beside the point, so we had to pivot and make it right.

Keep in mind, I was driving through the mountains to Montana for Thanksgiving while I was trying to rectify this horrible experience for our guests and considering how I was going to deal with how it happened later. So the solution was to apologize profusely and then suggest that they go into town to grab some drinks or dinner and to let me know where they ended up so that I could call in and pick up their tab. The tab ended up being $300, which wasn't ideal, but the house got a proper cleaning and they were still able to enjoy their Thanksgiving trip at the beach. Plus, the cleaners did not charge me for that cleaning, given the circumstances, and the momentary problem was solved. Sigh of relief!

What wasn't resolved was how that miscommunication happened in the first place. At this point, I really hadn't ever checked the cameras because we didn't have any issues or need to until then, which was wonderful. The fact that we could go back and check the cameras and the door sensors was a huge help in defining the issue. Ultimately, we never found out exactly what happened, but it was not a squatter, thankfully. The cleaner had come to the house late at night but left after a short amount of time, less time than it would take to clean the house. No other comings or goings had gone on. So, basically, some guests checked out, the cleaner came late and maybe did some cleanup or assessment, and then they left and never returned. The house manager never got it communicated to her that the house was not ready, which meant that the next guests checked in to a very unpleasant surprise.

This led to an important lesson in self-management, which is to get a security system with a code that only YOU know, not even the house manager. So, my new protocol, especially during the slower seasons, is to set the alarm controlled from my phone after the house has been turned over so that the cleaners or house manager need to let me know when they are going by and only I can disarm the alarm for them. I also highly recommend having door sensors in the event that your cameras are down so that you can at least see when doors are opened and which ones have been accessed.

This is a way to control the comings and goings of everyone involved. Also, everyone knows that they can't just show up at any time without letting you know ahead of time. You want to remain in control, make sure that everything is on the up and up, and be assured that your employees know that you are closely monitoring the property. It just keeps everyone honest.

The door locking system is your next line of defense to keeping your property secure between guests and vendor visits. You want one with a code that can be changed from a distance. Generally, the house manager or cleaning crew will have another code and then guests will get their own personalized code for their stay. There are a few different Wi-Fi options on the market and it is a good idea to change the code after every stay. Some Hosts don't change the code after every stay but sporadically throughout the year. It is whatever your comfort level is. We air on the side of caution and change the code after every guest. Our one close call with a supposed squatter is all we need!

To tie this all up in a bow, when many people think of self-management, they think that it means you are the boots on the ground, cleaning the property and turning it over between guests. In reality, it can be a remote job. Time and time again, people ask if I self-manage and when I say, "Yep!" then they are shocked. They usually respond, "Wow, that is a lot of work." It is work, but there is more to managing than just cleaning. It also does entail someone being the boots on the ground to get turnovers done and report on the condition of the home, furnishings, and supplies. My way of self-managing is pretty hands-on, but there is room for you to delegate more of the guest communications and listing management than I personally prefer to. Rest assured that each aspect of this process can be tailored to whatever works for you!

Chapter 14:
Ready to Launch

Welcome to the launch phase. You made it! So, now you are ready to launch your listing. Well, kind of. You are ready to pre-launch, which is a critical phase of my launch formula. A pre-launch is where you stay in the home yourself, ideally with some friends or family so you get unbiased opinions that will likely be more positive than your own because you are too close to the project and details at this point. After you stay there yourself for a couple of nights, you will learn how things actually work, what is comfortable, what isn't comfortable, and what necessities you should add before real guests stay there.

After you stay there on your own with friends the next phase of your pre-launch is to have people stay there without you. You can charge them a super discounted rate or maybe just charge them the cleaning fee, but ultimately you will have a group of guests come to stay that reaches your home's capacity limit. Make sure that whoever you offer this deal to will actually give you honest feedback without unnecessary nitpicking. These guests can be friends, family, or co-workers, but this phase is critical as a test run before you go live on the platforms and have strangers experience your home.

Then, allow yourself the time to add things that you need to include, change anything that needs to be adjusted, and take care of last-minute repairs that you didn't realize were needed. Have your cleaners come back through so they can get it turned over like they will once it is listed so you can experience their work and give them the necessary feedback.

Now you are media ready! When it comes time for your professional photographer to come over, I recommend being present or having someone there who knows your overall vision. You will want your bedding and furniture to be just as you intend it to be before the photographer arrives. Since this will also help your cleaning crew carry out your vision between guests after things get moved around, this is a visual training tool as well.

The photographer will be taking still photos, drone shots, and video both inside and outside of your house and then shooting pictures of area attractions and amenities as well. You will also want some detailed shots of furnishings and lifestyle moments so that guests can really envision themselves being there from your listing photos. Many guests also really like it when a floor plan is provided. It usually takes a few days to get all of the media back, so this is a great time to be working on the listings on your various platforms in draft mode.

When it comes to various rental platforms, there are really two that stand out—Airbnb and VRBO. Of course, if you talk to property management companies, they will say that they list on hundreds of sites, but in reality these two are the big ones. In my personal opinion, Airbnb is the most user-friendly for both Hosts and Guests. I would say that the majority of my bookings come from Airbnb with VRBO being a close second. Another option for guests is for them to book directly on a property website, but this only really comes into play after someone has stayed at the property and knows what they are looking for, or they know you personally and are familiar with your rental. So, when it comes to getting your investment booked while streamlining things, these are the two platforms I focus on.

Each platform will lead you through its listing process. As a Realtor by day, this type of program is something that I am already used to. What I know is that descriptions sell, especially when it comes to vacation rentals. Prospective guests want to know exactly what to expect for their stay, so you want to describe every floor of the home including each bedroom and bathroom, the accessibility options, the kitchen amenities, the home features, and the nearby attractions. Your Guest Guide will be an extension of your listing and available during their stay, but your listing is what hooks them to book them.

Your title on each platform should be keywords that will entice someone to click on your listing and include a captivating photo of your property. You may also refer to the home by its name. When going with a name, you should use it with your vendor team as well as with guests. For example, the names of our homes are Anchor14, Lighthouse13, and Vista Ridge, all of which come from their location and the market theme.

Then there is good ol' social media. I use Instagram to showcase and promote our properties to people that I already know and to people who are interested in that type of vacation or location. I include the Airbnb links in my bio so that people can click in there, check out the properties we have, and see their availability for booking. Aside from the property links being available, I like to bring people along for the behind the scenes of short term rental life. This takes the experience beyond the listing photos and shows what it is really like to vacation at the property and visit the attractions that we enjoy while we are there. It is also a great place to showcase those glamorous professional photos and spotlight all of your rave reviews!

Instagram is also a great place to review local favorites—restaurants, beaches, rental shops, events, and so on. Then, when you add your IG handle to the marketing section of your Guest Guidebook, current guests can go and check out your account to get the most updated information on the area.

The long and the short of it is that social media can be a great tool for boosting your investment's success and encouraging your guests to connect with your property online during their stay. Honestly, I hope you name your property early on and start getting followers during your buying and prepping process. Get people excited about your new adventure, your new house, and your guests' new vacation opportunity!

The internet is your main—or, dare I say, only—source of bookings, so you need to look damn fine online. Don't skimp on how things look in person. I don't mean that it needs to be high-end. Just keep it comfortable, clean, and photo ready. The way it photographs and shows online will be the difference in how many bookings you get. Make sure to showcase all of your amenities. Also, keep in mind that you want the photos to be accurate. You don't want your property to look drastically better online than it does in real life. No one wants to be catfished, especially while on vacation.

As I mentioned earlier, Airbnb and VRBO will walk you through their listing process, so you will just need to follow their prompts. The final product will be your listing. Be prepared to write an overall property description, room descriptions, locations of bedrooms and bathrooms, and entry types. You will also describe whether you offer a shared space or an entire house rental and if there are any of the following: office space, gym equipment, shared or private pool, hot tub, security system, and certain interior amenities like hair dryer, shampoo, toilet paper, etc. It will be a lot of information and it usually takes me an hour or so to make sure that I don't miss anything.

This will also be the point when you choose one of the cancellation policies that they offer and determine your nightly rate. I will talk about pricing again later on, but when you are up to this point you likely already have a price point in mind. You will also have an opportunity to allow their online rate tool to decide for you. I personally have always opted to set my own price because I feel comfortable valuing properties since I do that for a living. Our homes are usually superior to the competition, so their pricing tool that works just like a Zestimate will leave money on the table for us. These algorithms don't take into account the finishes and location amenities. Instead, they just cover the hard data, which does not tell the whole story or provide an accurate depiction of value.

While you are building out your listings, you can preview them in draft mode and check everything for accuracy along the way. At the same time, don't get too stressed about it because you can always edit it, even after the listings are live. Your biggest draws for getting your first bookings will be your headline, description, and photos. Your pricing will also dictate how many people are searching for a property like yours, so you may want to start on the lower end of your range to get those first few bookings going.

Once your listings are live, go back to social media and share them with the world! You can even offer a discount for your followers to get more people engaged. People will be excited for you and for their new vacation spot.

Can you believe it?! You are now officially a Host. Congratulations!

> Get my listing verbiage from the QR code!

Part 3:
Let's Make Some Money

Chapter 15:
Managing Reservations

Welcome to the chapter that you will want to reference time and time again. Here is where you will learn all of my tactics for managing guests. I will cover reservations, the calendar, pricing, different platform nuances, guest guides, rules, protocols, and general communication with guests. It is a boatload of information and I can't wait for you to see behind the scenes, so let's GOOOO!

Reservation Management Systems:

When it comes to reservation management, you will handle those requests via different "channels." A management channel is how public platforms are referred to on a third-party management system. I happen to use iGMS to control all of our listings on the two major platforms, Airbnb and VRBO, but I didn't start with a third-party system. Initially, I just went directly between Airbnb and VRBO to keep up with reservations and guest communication. When we got our second investment, I knew it was time to streamline things and iGMS was the system I chose. However, when you are just managing one property, I think it is doable to handle them on the platforms themselves, especially since the calendars sync with each other so that you avoid double bookings between the two sites.

Guest Communication:

Reservation management is all about the initial communication with the guest and making sure that the cleaning crew or necessary vendors are aware of when they need to be at the property to turn it over or service something. Another reason I switched to the iGMS system was so that I could easily add my cleaners to the properties and that they could login to see when their next cleaning day would be, which also helped cut down on our back-and-forth communication. They could easily stay on track without confusion or waiting for me to tell them. You can add a co-host on Airbnb and VRBO, which functions similarly if you aren't ready to commit to a third-party management system.

When you have your calendar full of reservations, then you need to figure out how to communicate with your guests. Initially, when I just had one property, I would immediately message them in addition to the app confirmation message to ask for their email so I could send them an electronic version of the Guest Guide. This was before you had the ability to build guest guides directly on the apps and platforms themselves.

Then, on the morning of their reservation, I would send their door code and any important information. I quickly realized that I needed to automate this system. A great way to do this is to either build email templates, have the instructions saved on a Google doc, or build the templates available on Airbnb, VRBO, and iGMS, or other management channels as they are referred to. Each has its own version of automation. If you use just a couple of platforms and have just one property, you can easily do the automation for each app. If you end up going with a channel manager management system like iGMS, you can build the automation for each property in one place.

Things that I include in this message are, obviously, the door code and also, especially if your property is remote, the pin link if GPS won't get them there easily. I send instructions on how to use certain things, like our high-tech shower in one of our houses. I now include our check-out instructions out of the gate so they have it at the top of their message, inside the home as a printed version, and through the listing. That way, they aren't scrambling on the day of check-out to figure out what needs to be done upon departure. And, of course, I also ask them to notify me if something isn't as they expected upon arrival, since that is the best time to rectify any issues!

To Auto-Book or Not To Auto-Book?

The big consideration when it comes to reservation management is whether to allow auto-booking or not. A lot of people who rent their personal homes have a hard time doing auto-booking because they want more information before they rent to someone. Those who do this primarily for an investment, however, are incentivized to have it set up to auto-book.

Your listing will come up higher in the search feed and on social media advertisements when your auto-book feature is turned on. The way it works is that as long as the calendar has availability, the reservation request will be accepted. You may want to do this because your listing will get boosted on public platforms. You get rewarded as a Host for guests to be able to book your place without waiting for you to confirm. Keep in mind that it isn't totally the Wild West; they still have to provide the required documentation that you set up for your listing before it can be accepted. This is a personal preference, but it should be known that the listings that have auto-book turned on will get more bookings.

House Rules:

While you are thinking about which type of Host you are going to be, an auto-booker or not, you will also want to be thinking about your general house rules. These will be determined based on your preferences, concerns, housekeeper's requests, and property amenities. House rules include anything from check-in and check-out times, check-out cleaning instructions, and areas of the house that are closed off to guests to rules about using the hot tub, fireplace or fire pit, pool, bikes, and boats.

My personal opinion is to give your guests the benefit of the doubt but to make sure that they have all the information they need to be a great guest that you would welcome back. If you don't want people using the fireplace, then they should know that clearly and you should not leave out any of the items that they would need to use it. If you need them to load the dishwasher and run it prior to checking out, then they should have a reminder by the sink. If you need them to do laundry before they leave, make sure to send the check-out instructions the afternoon before they leave so they have time to prepare.

At the same time, don't make it overwhelming and overbearing. Yes, you are inviting people to stay in your home and you may feel the need to assert as much control as possible, but you want people to feel welcome and comfortable, not like a hostage in your home. I keep the rules basic. Check-out instructions are in the kitchen. They get the house rules in the Guest Book and electronically through the app. Maybe I am lucky, but overall we have had respectful guests who also report issues or things that get broken so we can be proactive. My cheeky write-up on house rules will be shared at the end of this chapter.

I like to keep our house rules fair, clean, and a little fun. I personally hate when I check into a vacation rental and I feel like I am walking on eggshells the whole time with all of their crazy rules and threats of fines.

I put good rental juju out there and so far, so good. Yes, people have broken things, things have disappeared, and guests have been messy, but it's just part of the gig. People are going to be people and this is an element of this type of investment. Lean into it and try to do your best to create a space that can handle this sort of environment.

When Guests Break Things:

It is going to happen and it is okay! You shouldn't have put anything in your house that you would be crushed if it got broken or went missing. I am very upfront with my guests that accidents happen and that is okay! You just need to let me know ASAP so I can make sure that things are replaced for the next guest. You can charge people for items that need to get replaced or you can just call it the cost of doing business. Whatever your comfort level is totally fine. You just want to be neutral when these things happen so that it does not backfire when they go to leave you a review. If it was really that awful or if they were disrespectful of your space, there is insurance through the various platforms to cover you and you can always leave a rating in the review process to state that you would not host them again.

If you are mentally prepared going into it, hopefully, you won't be emotionally charged when something does break or go missing. You should come up with a protocol for what happens when 'x'. So, if something gets broken, how will you approach it with the guest? What will you charge them? I have found that they are usually pretty respectful about reporting broken items because they are fearful that they will get charged after check-out anyway. You can charge them for items through Airbnb and VRBO if something does arise. For example, I have had a full area rug ruined and the guest fessed up to it before check-out, so I was able to charge them through the app to get it replaced with ease.

Pet Policy:

Most people are very happy to be able to bring their pet and are respectful. It also gets you more bookings by allowing pets, so we have always opted to allow them and to charge an additional fee. We also personally have pets, so we get it. There is a market for homes that don't allow pets and never have allowed them, but the demographic appears to be smaller than the pet lovers in our experience and markets.

The way I handle it is to charge a flat fee for the duration of their stay for up to 3 pets. With our beach properties, we tend to have people with multiple dogs staying in our homes. The additional fee just makes it a non-issue with any additional cleaning or cleaning time that happens on the back end. It is a great way to pad your repair fund as well. As you read earlier, I also ask guests to bring their own pet bedding and towels. We do have dog bowls, but we ask that they don't allow their pets on any furniture, bedding, or linens. We have enough laundry to do and can't add more to the list, as requested by our cleaners.

Check-in and Check-out Times:

I never had any idea how this was determined until I became a Host and learned that those times really are determined by the housekeeping crew. When it comes to our one market, our housekeeping crew is so busy that we had to move our check-in time back to 4 or 5 pm and we kept check-out at 11 am. This was also dictated by the size of our homes and their overall capacity. Since our homes all sleep around 10 people, that is a lot of laundry to turnover and it just takes time. Especially in the high season with same-day turns, it was impossible for our cleaners to get the house properly turned around before 4 pm. However, whenever I can, I try to give people early check-in and late check-out. It is solely determined by whether we have someone coming in later in the day or not and the cleaners' workload for that day.

Guest Guide:

With most things being digital in this day and age, it feels a little silly to have a printed copy of your guest guide in the home, but I find that guests really do appreciate it. This is your moment to throw in additional information that you wouldn't want to share over the app such as adventure recommendations, restaurants, attractions, shopping, etc. I try to keep my app instructions simple and straightforward so they don't miss anything, but I also have them readily available. If they want recommendations, they can reference the book in the house or they can message me directly for specific information.

I also recommend that you have an electronic copy that you can send to the guest ahead of their arrival. However, some management companies send so many emails prior to your stay that don't really pertain to your reservation that I find annoying, so I avoid sending along more clutter. In the home, you should have a printed and laminated version of the guest guide so it withstands multiple guest stays. This should be where all the house rules are kept along with Wi-Fi info, local emergency contacts, and places to eat, drink, shop, and visit. I also include my contact info and my house manager/cleaners' info, and then I invite them to tag our Instagram account. This should set you and your guest up for success with fewer messages during their stay!

Pricing:

Now for a little bit of art and science: Pricing. There are website tools that you can use to price your property, or you can leave it up to the app with their auto-pricing tool. Maybe this is the Agent in me, but I rely on my own market research and comparisons to arrive at my nightly pricing. All of my pricing varies throughout the year, but my weekend and holiday prices are higher than my weekday pricing. And my peak season pricing is higher than my low season pricing. I tend to go six months out at a time to price stays, and then adjust as the season arrives to make sure the calendar is filling up.

As long as your market has demand, you will be able to tell if your pricing is accurate or not. You want to get the peak season fully booked, but if it isn't getting booked then you need to lower your pricing. I tend to start on the higher end a few months out and then adjust down as needed. I will also fill in the calendar gaps by lowering prices the week or month of to try to get it filled. No matter where your rental is, there will be ebbs and flows in pricing and demand. With our homes being some of the nicest and largest in our markets, I look at the highest-priced places for comparisons and make a decision based on that. I only have the calendar open for six months at a time and, if we aren't getting bookings, I will hop in and change the pricing to get things booked up.

There, of course, will be times of the year when your property is booked every day, others where it is booked at least every weekend, and some when you maybe only have five nights booked for the month. You need to understand the seasonality of your market, what prices you should start with, and what prices you should strive to hit.

Often, you will start with lower pricing in your first year or two of renting to get some bookings and good reviews. Once you have a good base of renters, you can start to creep your pricing up. You will also know what amenities you may need to add or what things guests are really enjoying about your property so that you can lean into those elements with your visual and verbal marketing on your listings to capture more of your ideal guest.

The only lesson I learned is to make sure that you keep up with the holidays and bump up your pricing for those dates. People will book those much farther in advance and you don't want to accidentally have it listed for your base price when you should be asking your top rate. I set a reminder in my calendar to revisit the pricing calendar before holidays arise to avoid this. I learned this one the hard way in our first year. Airbnb had applied a random lower rate for our property and I didn't yet understand how to use the platform or keep an awareness of being proactive about holiday pricing in advance. Then, I got distracted by other things and didn't revisit holiday pricing until a reservation was confirmed for Christmas for a deeply discounted price that was below our regular nightly pricing. Dang it! But it was a lesson learned and I haven't made that mistake again.

When it comes to managing your reservations, you want to be clear, fair, and helpful. People are waiting on you for guidance on how to get to your property, how to get in, and what is expected of them. With technology, it is quite easy to streamline the basic needs of your guests. As far as pricing goes, you will just have to do some trial and error. The good news is that you can always adjust the price, which you may have to do more of in your first year in order to get traction and understand the true demand versus pricing relationship in your market. Don't be afraid to jump in and figure it out along the way. No one will be able to give you a definitive answer on where to price your property for the best results. This is where the art and science combination comes in again. The same goes for your house rules and communication systems. You will have to just start, see what works or what doesn't work, and improve along the way. You are, after all, embarking on an entrepreneurship role, so it will take a bit of research and tinkering to hit the sweet spot. You can do this!

As promised, our house rules:

Check-in: Easy virtual check-in
Your personal door code will be provided to you before your arrival. This code will be changed immediately upon check-out. Check-in is at 5 pm unless otherwise arranged.

Wi-Fi: Network Name
Password: Goes Here

Parking: No street parking.
All vehicles must be in the driveway or garage during your stay.

Quiet hours: 10 pm-7 am
We like our neighbors, so please keep your merriment under control past 10 pm. We do have security that patrols in the evenings.

Amenities: Make yourself at home!
We love hosting guests, and want you to be just as comfortable at [House Name] as you are at home, or even more so. If it's here, feel free to use it. Just make sure to return it in the same condition as you found it.

Accidents happen: Don't sweat it! But please do tell us.
We have all broken a glass or a plate, it's no big deal, but please let us know so we can replace it for our next guests. Any damaged property, furniture, decor, or amenities will need to be replaced immediately, so don't delay in confessing your mishap :) Just send us a message through the app that you booked. If upon arrival something doesn't seem right, also report issues through the app. We will promptly respond. Thank you for your assistance!

Laundry: Available throughout your stay
There is laundry soap in the laundry room and you are welcome to do laundry as needed during your stay. We just ask you don't overload the machines and only run them while you are in the home. Please do not run the washer or dryer while you are away for concerns of flood & fire hazards.

Check out: Garbage, dishes, laundry, oh my!
Take all of your food and beverage remains with you or throw them out. Take out the garbage & recycling to the bins on the side of the home (left of the garage doors). Please pull back the covers on all used beds, so it is obvious they were occupied. Take all dirty towels to the laundry room and start a load of towel laundry. Load and run the dishwasher before departure. Make sure to lock up & turn off all lights by 11 am on your check-out date. We look forward to hosting you again soon!!

Fireplace & firepit: use with great caution & safety, please!
We love a good fire, which is why we are happy to have [House Name] equipped with a fireplace downstairs and a firepit in the backyard. Feel free to use them. We just ask that you use fire safety at all times. Must bring your own wood, and abide by local Burn Bans when necessary. Keep a hose nearby just in case. Please contact us with any questions.

Pets: We love our fur children, too!
We are happy to host your pets when you come to stay at [House Name]. In order for it to work for everyone, we just ask that you bring your own pet bed/bedding and towels. Please keep your pets off of the furniture and bedding, and only use our towels for humans :)

Beach towels: don't forget to bring them!
Due to housekeeping restrictions, we aren't able to provide beach towels. Please leave ours in the home and bring beach towels for your time on the sand.

Chapter 16:
You Are In Hospitality, After All

As I mentioned previously, guest communication is critical. Having great communication will make you a great Host. Guests want to know what to expect without being overwhelmed. If you have your auto-booking feature turned on, then your first communication with them will be after the platform already accepts and confirms their reservation for you. So, your next step will be to reach out with "welcome" information.

I have noticed personally and with our own guests that if guests feel connected to a friendly host, then they tend to be respectful and friendly in return. When someone thinks they are renting from an investor or huge management company that can't be bothered to communicate with them organically, it can negatively impact their experience and, in turn, the result of their stay. Personally, I think it really pays off to act as an engaging and personable host.

So, how do I do this? Well, I touched on it in the last chapter with my example of our Guest Guide House Rules. I like to keep communication upbeat and fun. If you can make a joke in your house rules instead of the regular stuffy demands, your guests will feel more comfortable in your space and when reaching out to you, should they need to during their stay. It is also crucial to be available to reply to messages from them within a couple of hours. Nothing is more infuriating than needing assistance during your stay and not getting a response or getting a response but not getting the issue resolved. I can absolutely say that my responsiveness and friendly communication have landed us great reviews, even if a guest has had a sizable inconvenience that directly relates to our property.

For instance, we had a washer and dryer go out during one of our first reservations for guests who were on a multiple-week road trip. We were their first homestay instead of a camping stay in many days, so the washer and dryer breaking was not great in general and definitely not for these sweet folks banking on the opportunity to wash their clothes. I responded immediately and was able to get our handyman out there to get them repaired enough to work during their stay. Crisis averted! We also ended up replacing these appliances shortly after this because that was embarrassing for our brand new listing to have a major malfunction like that! In the end, they gave us a 5-star review despite their trouble. I wholeheartedly attribute that to my responsiveness and willingness to get someone out to fix it ASAP.

I have personally stayed in places where something breaks and it is a lengthy process to submit your request, let alone get it resolved during your stay. Excuse me, what!? A prime example was when we were renting a large home with a hot tub for a family vacation with all the cousins. We arrived and the hot tub didn't work, so we called to get it tended to. They told us that they knew it was broken and that it needed a new part.

Being a host myself, I was not pleased. First of all, because we specifically booked a home with a hot tub and, second, because they knew about it but did not let us know before we arrived or after we booked. After our stay, we did end up getting a discount, but all of that could have been avoided from the start. It also left a bad taste in our mouths about the management company. Needless to say, you are in hospitality! You are in the business of making sure that people enjoy time away and spend their hard-earned money on your space. It is your job to make sure they have as lovely a time in your property as possible!

So, how do I stay in touch with these people and respond so quickly? I primarily communicate with Guests via the app they booked on or through our channel manager account. This cuts down on confusion for you and for them, keeping it all in one place. You will remember that I communicate when they initially book and then I communicate on the day of check-in to deliver them the code, any pertinent information, and check-out instructions. I also ask them to let me know if anything isn't as they expected upon arrival. Nothing is more frustrating as a Host than getting a poor review at the end of a stay for something that could have been addressed at the beginning of their stay. Your vendors are human. Things can get overlooked or missed, so it is much better to be able to make it right immediately instead of hearing about it later.

Other than that, guests will reach out to me with questions before or during their stay. I try to respond to them immediately, which I know may sound crazy or impossible depending on your lifestyle, schedule, and availability. However, it is second nature to me as a realtor because I am used to responding to people via text, email, and phone call at all hours of the day every day of the week. So, I realize that this could be a hurdle for someone who isn't used to so much ongoing communication, but it is actually pretty easy to manage. The messages come into your phone on the app and you get notified right away. It is as simple as responding to a text but through the app. Sometimes it has taken me a couple of hours to respond, but, for the most part, it is pretty instant. I do get feedback on how appreciated that is and, if this is part of the management that may not fit with your schedule, then that may be something you outsource to your house manager or another vendor or assistant.

With all of the things I do right with our investments, I also can't make everyone happy. There will always be someone who just isn't going to be satisfied, no matter what you do. Or they will be a harsh critic of space, design, etc. for whatever reason. It doesn't happen often, but it does happen. For me, I handle these things on a case-by-case scenario. Generally, you can just ask people what resolution they are seeking and come to an agreement. YOU ARE IN HOSPITALITY. So, making it right, instead of being right is going to serve you much better.

However, if someone is being extremely unreasonable or emotional, you do have the right to stand your ground. You just want to make sure your guests are taken care of. This is certainly a business that can require moments of gritting your teeth and bearing it to avoid a bad review. In this day and age, your online presence and reviews are going to be something people consider heavily when they are deciding to rent your place or not. So, sure, shit happens that you can't control and sometimes people won't give you grace, but I do fully believe in staying positive, calm, and accommodating when it comes to handling your guests. The gift in dealing with an unhappy guest is to realize that some pain points in your process or amenities will be able to make it better for future guests.

My point is that the attitude of welcoming someone into your home and having the perspective of "the customer is always right" is the best way to handle each guest and any challenges that arise. If you run into too much trouble, then that would be a moment in time when you should regroup with your house manager, cleaners, or whoever is involved to make sure that the same situation does not occur in the future.

Trust me, the Thanksgiving fiasco of 2022 was not great. I was horrified, frustrated, and embarrassed, as well as confused. But the $300 bar tab was worth it because I also wanted to make sure I could do whatever was in my power to rectify the start of their holiday from being

Chapter 16: You Are In Hospitality, After All

derailed. In the end, all was well. I fully believe that the approach I take to managing guests and problems keeps them from spiraling out of control. If you lead with a mindset of hospitality, you will build a business that will stand the test of time and bring in guests who come back to your property time and time again. Mission accomplished!

Chapter 17:
From Zero To Superhost

If you want to maximize your investment's success, then you will want to aim to hit the prized metrics set by the rental platforms. These achievements will fetch you higher occupancy rates and top pricing by landing you more exposure on their websites. Luckily, unlike some platforms, their algorithm and metric qualifications are fully disclosed and tracked for you. The success of these sites lies in the hands of successful hosts like you!

What are the metrics to become a Superhost on Airbnb or a Premier Host on VRBO? Both platforms have their own set of expectations, and Airbnb has higher standards than VRBO to maintain this elite status. For all of our properties, we have been able to achieve and maintain Superhost and Premier status since the get-go. So, what are these elusive awards and how do you achieve them?

Airbnb Superhost:

Every 3 months, your listing will be evaluated to see if you've met the Superhost criteria for the past year. If you do, you'll maintain your Superhost status. This means that every three months, you can qualify for Superhost. You don't have to wait a year to get this status and your goal as a new listing should be to hit these metrics to make your listing a success from the start.

+ Your overall rating will need to be a 4.8 average or better
+ Your response rate to inquiries needs to be 90% or better
+ You will need to have 10 completed stays or 100 nights booked over 3+ reservations
+ Your Host cancellation rate needs to be 1% or less

Airbnb also provides Airbnb Coupons to their Superhosts for achieving that status and for the length that they maintain that award. I have been a Superhost for over a year, so they gave me $100 to use on a personal stay at another Airbnb listing of my choice. Our listings get promoted when Guests search on the platform and, with the Superhost badge, Guests can search for listings that only have the Superhost status. You also get access to a ton of resources and support through the website or app.

VRBO Premier Host:

Similar to AirBNB, VRBO assesses the Premier Host status every 3 months by reviewing your combined performance from the last year. That being said, if you meet the new criteria sooner, you'll automatically gain acceptance across all your listings. Their criteria are as follows:

+ Average Rating: 4.3 stars
+ Acceptance of Reservations: 90% or better
+ Accepted Bookings: 5 per quarter or 60 nights in a year
+ Total Reviews: 3
+ Cancellation Rate: Less than 5%

There are definite differences between the qualifications, but ultimately you want bookings with great reviews during every three-month period. This means that you need to focus on all of the things that we covered in this book so far—comfort, amenities, accurate pricing, and availability. This is a beauty pageant with a side of pricing science. Your listing needs to grab the attention of the most people searching in that area for a price that is on point with the market.

Keep in mind, you will also need to adapt to your Guest's needs, but sometimes negative feedback about how the property is set up is a personalized problem and not a generalized problem. What I mean by this is that the guest may comment that the bed wasn't comfortable. Okay, so noted. This is something to keep an eye out for. But, has anyone else commented on that? No; on the contrary, they ask what the mattress brand is because it is so comfortable. So, this tells you that the complaint was just a one-off and goes back to the fact that you can't make everyone happy. Your goal is to make the majority of guests happy, as in, 4 stars or better happy.

This all ties into everything that you've learned so far. When it comes to our listings, we made them attractive and updated so that they photograph well, are comfortable, and have the ability to sleep a larger group than the majority of our competitors. This gives us an edge when it comes to getting our homes booked consistently, which also puts us in a position to reach these qualifications.

Another strategy I use to make sure that I am on the right track is to price with this in mind and revisit our ideal guest's needs. For example, for our homes, it is most likely that they will be rented by two families and bring their kids and maybe a couple of dogs. In order to get the most bookings, we make sure it is set up for families, is pet friendly, and is priced with the idea that our area isn't super expensive. However, we are priced on the high end of our market because they can sleep more guests and, in turn, our bookings usually split the reservation fee between two households.

To further break it down for you, if two families are renting a house for the weekend at the beach in peak season, it won't be a big deal for each to pay $500 per household. In other words, this is a two-night getaway for ten people plus their dogs in a rental that is close to the beach with room to spread out and enjoy. It's hard to find a hotel for that price where you would be missing out on the space and the amenities.

Being conservative on pricing for the first year will help ensure that you hit the metrics to qualify for Superhost and Premier Host. Don't try to set records. If you price more on par with other listings in your market to make sure you are competitive, then you will get the most possible bookings in your first year.

When we launched our first listing, it was during the peak season and we were booked almost every single day for the first three months. This made it easy to obtain the qualification regarding stays. Peak season is definitely something to consider further when you are building out your launch timeline. If you post your listing during a low season, you may not hit Superhost or Premier Host the first time around since you will not hit the number of qualifying stays.

Ultimately, what really drives your listing to obtain the ratings that you need to hit Superhost or Premier Host is your home's condition and cleanliness. Your cleaning crew is going to be the real MVP when it comes to getting good reviews. Whether it is home sales or rental stays, a clean home trumps almost any other flaw. Cleanliness coupled with being a friendly and responsive host means that you can't help but succeed!

People really just want a safe and clean place to vacation, so cleaning should be taken very seriously, especially if you are gunning for these coveted accolades. Cleaning is also one of the only major metrics that you can fully control, or at least your cleaners can. Your home is where your home is, and the location will play a role, but as long as you price it correctly, have a clean property, and are helpful for your guests, you will be able to achieve Premier and Superhost status.

Chapter 18:
Hosting Secrets For Lasting Results

Fourteen chapters of this book have been packed with all of the tactical ways that I successfully bought, launched, and continue to manage our short term rentals. One of the last tangible pieces of advice I will share is regarding the ongoing management of our properties. In my opinion, it comes down to quality control and being able to effectively manage your property. It is going to be critical for you to understand your property's quality as guests experience it. This is where those "work stay" visits come in handy. You will want to personally see how your property is turned over and presented for your arrival.

It is quite possible that, immediately upon arrival for your stay, you will notice all of the things that aren't as you left them or aren't as you expected them to be. This could range from small things to big things. For instance, it drives me nuts when I arrive at one of our properties and beds aren't made a certain way, furniture is in weird places, or the counters are cluttered. I realize that this can sound a little over the top. Like, chill girl. But I want our homes to look as they do in the photos because THAT is what your guest is expecting and, no matter what business you are in, you should deliver at least what is expected, if not better.

So, when you arrive and find things like this, it is a great opportunity to have a chat with the house manager or cleaner to discuss what the expectations are and to find out how you can help make it easier for the staff to execute it.

Out of this problem was born my solution to send the property link to the cleaners so they understand what I expect it to look like. It hadn't even dawned on me before that they had only seen it after a guest had been there when it was dirty! Duh. Of course, they had no idea that I wanted the beds made a certain way or the chairs in a certain location. Again, communication is key and that was my bad. From this point on, I can now reasonably ask that things be presented in a certain way. This also shows compassion and understanding for your house manager and for the challenges that they encounter. This is a prime example of the learning curve of a newbie STR owner.

So, what does it look like to prepare for one of these stays? When we are planning for these work trips, we generally have a lot of supplies to bring down, including the regular things that we are always restocking like shampoo, conditioner, lotion, toilet paper, paper towels, garbage bags, soap, etc. We also make a list of upgraded items that we either want to add to the property or because guests have mentioned it as something that would make the space better. We also have generally collected a list of things that need replacement and my husband has a list of repairs to do that are generally small. So, we pack up the kid, the dog, all the tools and supplies, and our bags for a few nights' stay in our vacation home.

Leading up to this trip, we have each made our own lists that fall under our responsibilities. I am the supply and replacement goods buyer. My husband is the repairman. I have also reached out to the housekeeping crew and house manager to see what feedback they have for us to be able to best prepare for the visit. Based on their reply, I come with everything we need to cut down on running back and forth to town for supplies, especially because the towns we own in aren't exactly bursting with options. Prior to this, I have also been making a list of guest comments as well, so if there is anything the cleaners or house manager haven't mentioned, I likely heard about it from a guest. All of this information makes for a productive trip.

On many occasions, we have taken off on a Thursday after work so we can get straight to work Friday morning and have friends come join us later in the weekend. That way, we get work done while also enjoying everything our home has to offer with friends. You can make it a trip for work and for fun! After all, you might as well enjoy this beautiful investment you have worked so hard on.

Now, the frequency of these visits will vary from person to person, depending on your proximity to the property and, of course, time availability. For us, we like to go and stay in our homes at least once a quarter. First of all, it is a great excuse to get away and, second, it is our chance to manage the quality of our property and assess any upcoming maintenance. It also allows us to keep an eye on how things are going in terms of cleanliness, reporting missing home goods by our vendors, and discovering any potentially unmentioned repairs. If you arrive and notice things that you would have liked to know about before you arrived, this is another great training opportunity.

In my case, most of my adult life has been spent in homes and attending home inspections, so I have extensive knowledge about what I am keeping an eye on for repairs and maintenance, but your house manager may not be as savvy in this department. So, take the time to explain to them what things they should be looking for and what to report back to you about. These homestays are meant to be working vacations and they are very informative from a management perspective. You will learn how your finishes are holding up, areas that your house manager can improve on their role, and how to strengthen your working relationship through better communication. Or maybe you find out that they are so stellar that you don't need to make any adjustments to their role. Winning! No matter what you find out, these visits are priceless.

Another reason that these visits are imperative for a successful investment is that you have the opportunity to follow up on reviews that may have mentioned some downfalls of your space or repairs that were needed. Make a list of the improvements that you have made, update your listing, and go back to reviews that mentioned those needs to let them know that you have addressed them and can't wait to host them in the future. This shows them you are an attentive Host and it shows prospective guests that you are proactively caring for your property, which gives them the confidence to book. Unfortunately, many properties don't get regular maintenance or don't address the issues that people mention in reviews. If people read your reviews and you have the same recurring issues, it will deter people from booking your place. Workstays with some intentional follow-up will go a long way toward the success of your investment.

From a marketing and advertising perspective, these stays are also very valuable to showcase your property to friends, family, and your online network by sharing about your time there. In my experience, people love two things—vacationing and real estate. Put the two together and they will follow along! This is your opportunity to show off all the fun and enjoyment that you can have by visiting your property. You can show the behind-the-scenes of the area and your personal favorite places to go, eat, and shop.

Plus, seeing you there makes it more relatable for others to want to book their stay, too. I like to take tons of photos that I can reuse on our social media account long after we have left the house. It is one thing to see glamorous professional photos, but people also want to see what "it really looks like." I often give my online followers a discounted booking option if they follow along and want to book directly through me because those people are also likely going to be your raving fan guests who will want to come back time and time again and also tell other people about it.

I love the platforms because it makes managing reservations quite simple, but getting more localized traction is a huge perk as well. I have a family from our hometown that has booked one of our beach rentals numerous times! They are wonderful and always give great, honest feedback about anything that may need attention, which is super valuable for us to prepare for our next work stay! If you have goals for growing your investments through multiple short term rentals, I recommend building an online presence early. People love to follow along for the journey.

So, are you sold on work stays yet?? Because I am. They are the most valuable thing in self-managing your properties to help you continue receiving ample bookings and rave reviews.

Chapter 19:
The Mountains On Your Horizon

At this point, you have a ton of information that may be new or improved from the knowledge you had previously about becoming a short term rental investor, but you may still have questions, concerns, or obstacles that you just aren't quite ready to let go of.

The biggest hurdle with getting started as a short term rental investor at this point in your journey is mindset. You have to believe that you can figure it out once you start, you have to believe in the process and systems that I have laid out, and you have to believe that you are worthy of being a real estate investor. It is okay to have some fears, doubts, and concerns. You just shouldn't let those deter you from getting started. The only way for you to become a short term rental investor is to start and learn along the way.

There will be obstacles that you encounter when you go to embark on your short term rental investing journey. All the way through the process, there are opportunities for hurdles to pop up. It can take time to find the right property. For us, we needed two years of shopping to feel comfortable enough to pull the trigger. That was partially because we were also building our other businesses, so taking on another project seemed like a big leap. It was also partially due to being fearful of the unknown—so, yes, that feeling is valid and normal.

If you are still in a fear mindset at the thought of having people living in your house, sleeping in your beds, using your bathrooms, and potentially breaking things in your property, then you can probably safely decide that this isn't going to be the real estate investing vehicle that is right for you. People will be sleeping in your beds and using your property as if it is their own and things will get broken. Trust me, if this is the right fit for you, those things won't be a deterrent at all. The things that will be more important to you are a high monthly cash flow and a property that you get to enjoy with your family and friends. If the idea of those things is exciting to you, then this is for you.

For me, I have always leaned on education from other investors online such as those on BiggerPockets and people who came before me to borrow their strength and wisdom to get on the same path as them. I do not ever want to reinvent the wheel; I would much rather see how the wheel is made and then optimize it into a process that is better and, more importantly, works for me. When I set out to embark on becoming a STR investor, I did not have a road map to follow. I gathered as much information from various places as I could and then used my own logic and life experiences to come up with a plan. Luckily for you, I am here to be your motivator, mentor, and peer in the real estate investing space.

It will take work and a certain level of risk tolerance, but the benefits can be beautiful and blissfully rewarding. The first time that you get to bring your friends on vacation to your top-producing rental is a magical feeling. The first time that you get a month of five-figure cash flow or enough rental income to cover your property for the next six months is a euphoric milestone in your investing journey. Just make sure to keep those funds in your bank account to save for a rainy day or your next short term rental purchase. The security and enjoyment that your short term rental can provide is second to none in the real estate investing world.

Chapter 19: The Mountains On Your Horizon

When you do find the right property that feels good for your goals and financial situation, then your next obstacle could be getting the property closed. Things could come up during the inspection that weren't foreseen and negotiations might not go as easily as you hoped. Just keep in mind that your Agent will be your guide during that phase. I also highly recommend that you keep the big picture in mind. The transaction is a small piece of your overall goal, so don't get hung up on something that will be insignificant in the days, weeks, or months to come.

After you close on your home, you're super excited, but your contractor that was going to help with the repairs and renovations could flake, be delayed, or not deliver on the projects they were hired to do. Nothing is more frustrating. But, guess what? It happens all the time, and there is always a solution. You can always hire someone else and the lesson you learned during that process will be so valuable to you as you move forward.

This may be your first go at hiring. Trust me, it is entirely possible that you could make the wrong hire, not communicate their duties clearly, decide that they are not as qualified for the role as they portrayed, or find out that the two of you just aren't on the same wavelength when it comes to hospitality. These things will happen. You will make a bad hire, someone will quit or retire, and you will need to hire again. As long as you understand that many of these functions of your business will be recurring, you will be fine and you will get better each time around.

You will encounter a guest that isn't happy. Your place isn't clean enough, this thing is broken, that amenity would have been nice to have, you were late on getting them their door code, or they just are the type that complains. Unfortunately, you will encounter guests like that. It is just a part of life and you can't make everyone happy.

Luckily, I generally have kind guests who are just so pleased to be away for vacation. Don't let the grouchy ones shake your confidence.

You should, however, take into account any of their gripes and examine your process and property to either improve those areas or determine it was a guest problem but not a property problem.

Or you could run into something crazy like a pandemic in the middle of your project—let's hope that never happens again in our lifetime—where supply issues are abundant and cause you a delay or force you to face constantly changing regulations. Do you know what is cool about unforeseen issues? Creative solutions! Life is unpredictable. What will make you a solid and successful investor will be your ability to adapt and pivot when needed. Change is constant—adapt.

No matter how well you set up your property, how well you run your business, how wonderful your vendors are, and how many precautions you take, problems will arise. You need to know that now, but if this is the right investment tool for you, that won't make you shy away. If anything, it should bring you comfort in knowing that this is happening to everyone that has a short term rental. As much as I try to pre-plan to avoid as many issues as possible, things come up. I always say that every type of investment will be a pain in the ass. You just have to pick the type of pain that you are comfortable with.

Maybe it is from my many years of residential real estate sales that I am accustomed to constantly being in problem-solving mode and communicating with clients at all hours every day of the week, but being a Host just does not bother me. Yet, I know people who like long-term rentals that could never imagine ever wanting to be in the short term rental business.

I personally enjoy the whole business of hosting just like I love the whole business of real estate sales. Neither of them is easy and both require a lot of effort, but I wouldn't trade them for another career path or retirement plan. If you want more out of life, you have to give more to the life you live.

Luckily for you, I have already lived a lot of this short term rental life for you so you can take all of my cheat codes and apply them to your own investing journey. If at this point, you feel like I just gave you enough information to be dangerous but you don't quite feel confident enough to conquer your first vacation rental alone, I highly recommend bringing in a partner. Whether it be a virtual partner or a hands-on partner, it can be a great way to get started or to grow.

I didn't talk about it much up until now, but sometimes strength in numbers is the best way to get going. Just as I have been a virtual partner to you through this book, you should seek the mentorship or education that you need in order to feel confident to take the leap. Oftentimes, you can find someone with the knowledge that is willing to do the brunt of the work if you put up the cash to buy the property or bankroll the build-out. Or maybe you have the knowledge and are willing to do the work, but don't have the money.

Jeff and I have not entered into any partnerships in our rental business outside of each other, but we have heavily considered it in the past. The keys to making it work with a partner are having an open line of communication, clarifying everyone's role in the partnership, and having a collective understanding of both the main goals of the partnership and the vision for the shared business. If at any point you are looking into a partnership and it doesn't feel quite right, then listen to your instincts and pass on the opportunity. It is much harder to undo a partnership than it is to turn down an opportunity that could end up being a nightmare.

QR Code: Tips on Partnerships

Chapter 20:
It's Time To Take The Reins

Do you feel ready to start your journey as a Host? I hope so. Real estate is a powerful and magical financial tool that can be approached from many different angles. Even if you have now decided that short term rentals aren't for you after reading this book, I am glad to have given you a peek behind the curtain so you know it doesn't sound like it would be a good fit for you. Or, maybe you are still interested in having a second home that you rent out, but you really don't want to self-manage it. Whatever the clarity is that you now have, I hope that it propels you in the direction that you should be heading in.

If you do decide to go down this path, then when you first list your property, you will be so excited, relieved, and nervous all at the same time. You will likely over-communicate with your first dozen guests. You will be so curious to hear their feedback and very hopeful that they have nothing but positive things to say. Once you get past your first five stays, I would say that you will start to notice a cadence and pattern for guest communication and feedback. Most will comment on the same positive features and some will leave private feedback for things you should improve.

At first, those improvement comments will feel heavy, but sometimes the feedback comments are very personalized. So, my wisdom is to not get too tied up in every bit of negative feedback because it may not always be valid for the masses. It also doesn't mean that you did something wrong or failed during your launch process. Just note that if you get the same feedback time and time again, then you need to make an adjustment.

An example of learning how to better improve our rentals was from our original short term rental. We kept getting feedback that the glare on the TV in the living room was bad because we had western exposure and the room didn't have blinds. It may sound odd, but the way that the house is set up, no one can see inside. To be honest, we never watch TV on vacation while at the beach, but the people spoke, so we installed blackout blinds and haven't had a comment about it since. Your guests will teach you what is important to them and it is your job as the Host to pivot and adapt as needed.

If you are looking to use my book as your guide to becoming a STR owner, then I highly recommend reading it through once, then read the *Buy* section when you are ready to start that phase of the process. Then, once you are under contract on your property, read the *Launch* section again and familiarize yourself with all of those tactical chapters. Once you are nearing your launch date, I recommend reading the *Manage* section to gear up for what is to come after your listing goes live. This will make sure you stay on track and don't get too far ahead of yourself while also understanding the overarching goal.

Most of all, I really hope that I have provided you with a ton of information and a framework to apply to your own hosting business. I hope that you feel empowered and educated to go out and start your own short term rental business. I hope you take the tools and resources that I have highlighted and make them work for you, your market, and your lifestyle.

Chapter 20: It's Time To Take The Reins

When it comes down to it, my overarching piece of advice is to just get started. You have nothing to lose because, if you remember, getting started just means doing some research—researching a market to buy in, connecting with a real estate Agent to help you get connected in that area, finding out from a lender or your bank what is financially possible for you and your situation, and then making a decision to shop or pivot. Once you start the shopping process, and you know the numbers, you just need to take the leap of faith, because you have all of the tools at your fingertips.

As I previously mentioned, I really wanted to write this book for you at this point in our journey because I feel that we are still at an attainable and approachable point in our short term rental business. I am not that much farther ahead than you even, if you haven't bought any real estate at this point. It can sometimes feel very out of reach to get coaching and guidance from someone who has 100 units, which also consist of hotels. Those people also forget what it feels like to start and to be new, including the thoughts, concerns, and problems that the newbie short term rental investor has. My mission is to make it clear that this is something that anyone can do, not just the wealthy or the savvy real estate investor. This is a dream and financial tool that you can absolutely attain.

I wrote this book because as soon as we started buying short term rentals, the number one comment I would get was, "I have always wanted to do that!" or, "I would love to have a short term rental—or multiple rentals." As I always say, "You can do this too! There is nothing extra special about us, aside from the fact that we will just do it." So, as I signed up for a book conference in the Fall of 2022 after a very rough year personally, I was planning to write a book for other real estate Agents. As I went through the coaching process, however, it was clear to me that I needed to write about our short term rental journey. So, here it is, the most approachable and tactical guide to becoming a successful short term rental Host.

Since we have gotten into short term rental investing, I have also helped others buy, launch, and manage their own properties and nothing has been more rewarding. As a matter of fact, I just got a text from some of our friends who bought their first vacation rental and they hit Superhost at their first metric milestone! It was such a meaningful message to get, given that I helped them buy the house and talked them through my whole process to get it ready, where to buy furnishings, what to have in the house, what the guest guide should say, who to hire, how to manage them, how to handle various guest situations, and then, of course, how to hit Superhost. They did the work; I was just there to mentor and guide them along the way. It was so impactful to see my process work for someone else.

So, here is to you as you embark on this new journey or continued journey of wealth-building to leave a legacy that is bigger than money. It is freedom, the opportunity to choose, enjoying life, spending time with loved ones, and providing a life full of more choices than have-to's. My wish is that this book opens doors to a life that you always imagined or never dreamed could be possible. My wish is that this sparks a new, positive trajectory for your life and your future. I hope that you find yourself feeling motivated to take the leap and do something more with your life.

My ultimate wish is that this book changed your life by giving you the push to jump into real estate investing in one form or another. I know for a fact that real estate is life-changing, so if my experiences gave you the encouragement to jump into the investor world, then my mission is accomplished.

Let's Connect:

www.soldonpaige.com/book
Instagram: @paige_sells_realestate
Email: book@thepaigemiller.com
Scan the Code For All My Free Resources or to Schedule a Call

Shout Outs

I want to take a moment to thank everyone who made this book possible.

First and foremost, my family—my husband, mom, sister, in-laws, and nanny. Without them to support this endeavor, I would never have been able to achieve this result, especially within a year. Thank you for everything you helped me with, from childcare for my days spent in Los Angeles with my book team to many hours spent after my normal workday in writing.

To my book team!! Jake Kelfer himself along with Cory Hott, Mary-Theresa Tringale, Meredith Edmondson, Elizabeth Horst, and Sohpie Hanks. The encouragement, the energy, the guidance, the coaching—it truly made this book journey attainable and fun. I was a complete newbie to the book-writing process and this dream team made it a wonderful experience.

And a huge thank you to my friends for their hype and cheerleading along the way. For asking questions, for encouraging me, and for getting excited for the book to be released—your involvement was crucial in getting the book produced!

Leave A Review!

So, what did you think?
I would love to hear from you in the form of a review!
This will also help others looking for this sort of content find this book. My mission is to help people learn about short term rental investing to see if it is the right fit for them and to encourage anyone who wants to get started to take the leap.
Help me do this by leaving a review on Amazon.

About Paige

By trade, Paige is a real estate entrepreneur—residential Realtor by day and real estate investor by night. She was born and raised in western Washington and grew up on the Puget Sound. Paige aims for continual personal growth all while achieving more in business and in life. Freedom is her main motivator and she loves to connect with other like-minded hustlers. Paige is married to her husband, Jeff, who is also her real estate investing partner. They have a sweet and sassy daughter, Amelia, who keeps them on their toes. Paige is also a crazy horse girl and loves to spend quality time with her horse, Vu. Family is the center of her world, so when she is not busy building in business, she is usually found spending time with them. She has been featured in Chicago Magazine and Top Agent Magazine for her achievements in real estate.

Follow along with all that she does @paige_sells_realestate or www.soldonpaige.com

Made in United States
Troutdale, OR
11/16/2023